Twenties in Your Pocket

A Twenty-Something's Guide to Money Management

By Kate Nixon Anania

ISBN: 9781731247650

This book is dedicated to Darius and Nicholas, my two favorite humans.

Table of Contents

Chapter 1: Your feelings

Empowered.

That's how I want you to feel after reading this book. Financial management isn't always fun or thrilling or sexy, but it is important and doing it properly can change your life. My wish for you is you will take what you learn from this book and feel empowered to line up your financial management with the goals you have.

Managing your money can be scary. It can be intimidating, it can be boring. You might feel guilty for not doing the "right" thing, and you might not even have any idea what the right thing is. People's feelings about money are complicated, and a lot of times money management comes with a lot of emotional baggage.

That's super normal. It's completely changeable. The fact that you picked up this book means you are already on the right track.

There is a lot to learn about money management, but none of that information is going to be helpful or useful to you if you feel nauseous any time you think about your finances. So our first step (bear with me, this really is a practical advice book) is to think about your current feelings about money and then think about how you want to feel about money in the future.

Here is a list of common feelings about money. Think about any additional words you might add:

- Stressful
- Scary
- Exciting
- An opportunity
- Boring

- Intimidating
- Provides security
- Overwhelming
- Fun
- Freeing
- Restricting
- Necessary
- Life changing
- In control
- Out of control

Some of these words are very negative— scary, boring, overwhelming. Some of them are positive— exciting, fun, opportunity. The difference between having negative feelings about money and having positive feelings about money is not about whether you *have* money, it's about whether you have taken steps to make sure your finances are helping you live the life you want. Even if you don't have a lot of money, you can still take steps to make sure your money supports your goals. You are probably going to spend a significant amount of your life working to earn money— let's make sure you know how to manage it so you can make the most out of what you have.

What do you even know about this?

Heya. I'm someone who had a super up-and-down financial decade in my twenties. I learned a lot and I want to share what I've learned with you.

I graduated college in May of 2008. I worked two jobs while in college, played a sport, earned good grades, had internships every summer, won awards and volunteered during undergrad. I did everything "right."

I spent the summer after I graduated volunteering at a position that would have turned into a job, except after

2

volunteering for the summer it had become clear to me the job was a horrible fit for me. I started job hunting in late September...exactly a week before the market crashed.

No one would hire me. At every interview I did, the employers all said the same thing, "A month ago we would have hired you, but now... we have a hiring freeze that may last a few years." I must have gone on 30 interviews. I wore out the lining of my interview suit.

I ended up patching together four (!) part time jobs for a year and I learned how to live on the cheap. Lots of libraries, beans, and box wine. The next year I got an internship and ended up living in a double wide trailer in rural Alabama, living on about $1200 a month. After that, I went to graduate school and lived on loans (and I got a degree in economics, so I do have official credentials to write this book). Then I got a-great-life-experience-but-not-very-lucrative-and-without-benefits fellowship. Finally, when I was 28, I got my first official job with benefits and a salary that meant I could afford guacamole on my burrito.

I am luckier than many. I had a fully funded undergraduate degree and I avoided credit card debt—but I also had to spent a lot of time scrimping and working side hustles and learning how to stretch what little money I had. When I was 22 and freaked out about being unemployed, I had no idea what a 401k was. I had never done my own taxes. I didn't know anything about money and I didn't know where to look. Financial management sounded boring and scary and so adult—but then I started learning a little bit. And then I started thinking about all the energy I spent to earn money. I thought I should be spending some of that energy to make sure my money is working the way I want it to. The more I learned, the better I felt and the more empowered I felt.

Here's how I feel about money: Excited. In control. Knowledgeable. Like it's an opportunity. Free. Empowered.

I wrote this book in case you are like I was. This book is for you. You can be empowered too.

How to read this book

In addition to getting a master's degree in economics, I also volunteer as a personal finance coach, write a blog and freelance articles about personal finance, and I teach classes to 18-30 year olds. My experience coaching and teaching has taught me people have hugely different understandings of personal finance. Some people don't really understand why banks are important while other people are interested in learning about how to manage their retirement investments. The first few chapters of this book cover the basics from the very beginning, but if you're finding you already know a lot of what I've written in the earlier chapters or the topics don't apply to you, feel free to skip around— I promise there is good information for you in here, too. If you want a quick and dirty workaround, I've put "Takeaway Actions" at the ends of each chapter.

This book is for you if you are:

- Intimidated by personal finance
- Worried about debt or overspending
- Just starting out in a career
- Thinking about college or graduate school
- Interested in making the most of what you have
- Unsure about investing or retirement accounts
- Relatively new to money management— my target audience is 18-35 year olds, but if you're just getting started at 45 this will work for you too!
- Bored by finance books
- Looking for a clear—cut guide to getting your finances on track
- Trying to lower money related stressors in your life

- Looking for information about how to manage money in a relationship

The point of this book is not to make you rich, but to manage what you have. Money can't buy happiness— at least not in the way loving relationships and fulfilling experiences can— but not having money can certainly contribute to unhappiness. The goal for this book is to teach you how to use your money so you don't spend your energy on financial worries, but instead use your money in ways that support what you want for your life.

Chapter 2: Banking basics

I once had a boyfriend who didn't believe in banks. And by he didn't believe in banks, I mean one day I came over and found him sitting on the bed surrounded by $30,000 in cash like Scrooge McDuck. I almost had a heart attack. For your personal safety and for the safety of your money, please do not keep all of your money in your home. Open up a bank account and welcome to adulthood— there are many perks here.

How do banks work?

Banks take their clients' money and they invest it. They don't physically have all of the cash that has been invested in them on hand. Clients get security (you don't even have to buy your own safe), access to cash (ATMs, bank tellers), checking services, and advice from real live bankers. Banks do a lot of other things too, like notarize forms and help with loans. Good banks will pay you some interest for putting your money into their system, and crappy banks will charge you fees so they can make more money even though they already make money off your money.

Banks are making money off you, and you get some things back in return. Plus, they are safe. Any bank you should feel good about using is insured by the Federal Deposit Insurance Corporation (FDIC). This sounds complicated but it really just means if your bank crashes the federal government will reimburse you up to $250,000. If your bank gets robbed, burns down or is hit by a tsunami, the money in your account is still fine.

There are a few factors to look at before you choose a bank. Here are the things to consider:

- Is it FDIC insured? Go to the FDIC website. They have a tool called "BankFind." If you can't find the bank on the FDIC website, it probably isn't a real bank. Do not give your money to any bank not listed on the FDIC website.
- Don't pay fees. Some banks charge fees and some banks don't charge fees. There is no reason why you should pay any "usage" fee or minimum deposit fee. If you are currently paying these fees or want to bank with a company that charges fees, call them up and ask them to stop charging the fees on your account, permanently. You can even find banks that won't charge you international currency conversion fees (Charles Schwab is the best!). Here is why you should feel fine about this: banks are using your money to make money they keep it safe for you. They should be paying you for the privilege of using your hard earned dough! And in fact, some banks will—through...
- Interest! Interest is my favorite thing to earn. You can find fee-free checking and savings accounts that will earn you interest. It won't be much, but free money is free money.

Shortcuts for picking a bank:

1. Type "no fee banks with interest earning checking and savings accounts" into your search bar.
2. Pick one. If it's listed on the FDIC website, you're good to go.

Types of bank accounts

So now that you understand banks, it's time to open up some bank accounts.

There are two main types of bank accounts you should be interested in: checking and savings.

Checking accounts:

- Although checks are not used much anymore, you'll still need to write them sometimes. This type of account allows you to easily write checks (hence the name *checking account*).
- This is the account you access with a debit card.
- You can access (most) of the money in this account almost immediately
- This account will usually give you a lower interest rate than a savings account.
- This account should be used for money you will need within the next six weeks (rent, beer money, car payments...)
- Try to find a bank that gives you free access to other banks' ATMs. Paying ATM fees is a waste of your hard earned money.
- Not to be too repetitive, but you should not be paying any fees for a bank account.

Savings accounts:

- This account is for money you will need within a year, but you won't need tomorrow. It takes a few days to move money in and out of your savings and there is usually a limit on how many transfers you can make per month.
- You will probably earn more interest in your savings account. It's not going to be a ton, but it will be more than in your checking account, and you should always have your money working for you.
- Savings accounts can be extra useful if you have student loans that are disbursed all at once but you need to make

them last for a whole semester— or if you get paid irregularly. You can set up an automatic transfer (poke around your bank website for this feature) so the amount you need for the month will move over to your checking account, where you will have access. It's like getting a regular paycheck...but you are earning a little interest (better than nothing) and you are helping yourself manage money so you can drink Rolling Rock instead of Natty Lite at the end of the semester.

- You can open up multiple savings accounts if you're saving for specific goals and you want to keep your savings for each goal separate.

Automatic bill pay

Now that you have bank accounts opened, you can discover one of the best lifehacks available for adults: automatic bill pay. If you've ever freaked out about losing your mail, forgetting a bill and especially if you've ever paid a gosh darn late fee, you should set up automatic bill pay. This is a service your bank will provide, and they will write a check every month for your rent, electric bill, phone bill...anything you set up. You can free up a ton of mental space by automating your finances. Sometimes you can set this up through your bank, and sometimes you have to set this up through the company you owe money to by linking to your bank. Either way, it's worth the ten minutes of setup to never have to worry about late fees.

Note: If you have variable expenses (like credit card bills) and you're worried about an overdraft, at least set up automatic bill pay to pay the minimum every month. That way you will never, ever pay a late fee.

A final thought: there might be a few things you want from your bank that you can't find with just one bank. It's ok to have multiple banks as long as you're organized. I have one bank for my checking account for the no fee international money exchanges, a different bank for my savings account because of the interest rate, and a different bank—actually a credit union—because it offers the best mortgage rates. I don't need a mortgage yet, but I keep a little money in an account there so when I'm ready to take out a mortgage I'll already be an established customer.

Emergency funds

Within your savings account system, you should have an emergency fund. I think having an emergency fund is even more important than paying down debt (although this depends on the interest rate and your credit limits), because emergencies do happen and not having the financial means to deal with them can make the situation significantly worse.

Here are some ridiculous things that have happened to me:

-I paid $75 to get my car emissions checked out in July (I had until the end of September to get it done). I sold my car in November. Apparently if your emissions inspection is over 90 days old when you sell a car you have to do it again. Doh! Paid $75 to get my emissions checked again in November...wah waah.

-I suddenly had a swollen, painful eye. Did you know you can have allergic reactions on the inside of your eyelid?!? Eye doctor appointment without vision insurance: $70.

-I got a letter from a state I had not lived in for a decade telling me I owed taxes on a car that I no longer owned. Since I didn't own the car anymore, I didn't have access to the paperwork proving I was off the hook... please enjoy my $120, you crumb bums.

All of these things were ridiculous and crappy and I was mad they happened to me and I was mad I had to spend money on them. I am sure you have an equally ridiculous list of things you have had to spend money on that you really didn't see coming (for your sake I hope I just have truly terrible luck and things like that don't happen to other people).

For me, the only good thing about these events was that I was able to pay for them. I was able to sell my car (which brought in a lot more than $75) — but I couldn't have sold it without paying for the emissions test. I still have two working eyes. I'm not a delinquent taxpayer, which could have hurt my credit and possibly my ability to get an apartment or even a job. See how all of these situations could have quickly worsened if I didn't have the money to deal with them?

The reason I could afford to fix these problems was not because I had any spare money. I actually had a huge amount of student loan debt and was eating beans every day, but within my budget I had an emergency fund. An emergency fund is a savings account you keep on hand for stupid, crappy emergencies.

Emergency funds aren't exciting but they save you from the only things worse than crappy expenses, and that is going into debt when you had to pay for crappy expenses that you didn't have money for.

Some guidelines for an emergency fund:

- Ideally, you should keep enough in your emergency fund to cover 3-6 months' worth of expenses. I know this may seem like a lot, but I have a few tips for how to get there. This will cover you for a bit in case you unexpectedly lose your job and it will give you time to get back on your feet. You may not even have any idea at this point how much 3-6 months' worth of expenses are, but I will cover that in chapter 4 so keep reading.

-It will take some time to save enough money to have a meaty enough emergency fund. Although other things will be more tempting (new phone, new shoes, basically anything else), try to prioritize saving until you have enough of a cushion.

-You should be keeping your emergency fund in a savings account. That means you are earning a little more interest than in your checking account, but you still have access to the funds within a few days. Don't count on your investments (more on investments later) as your emergency funds because there is no guarantee your investment will not be in a downturn when you need the cash most. A money market account is a great option— it's a savings account with a high interest rate that is FDIC insured, meaning you won't lose your money. Note: do not confuse with a money market *fund*, which is actually an investment account so you could lose your money. Another good choice is a high yield savings account, which should earn you the highest interest rates while still keeping your money safe.

-A separate savings account for an emergency fund is also helpful because it earmarks your money and helps you keep your finances organized.

-The best way to save for an emergency fund is to automate a transfer every month from your checking account into your saving account. Try starting with $25 a month if you're feeling intimidated.

-If you have a big change in life— get married, have a kid, get a new job— your expenses will change too. Make sure your emergency fund mirrors your spending. If you suddenly find yourself with more responsibilities (triplets!?) you might want to consider the six months' worth of expenses side of a safety net.

-The best part of an emergency fund? Once you have a cushion you are comfortable with, you don't have to build up your emergency fund further (though you will have to replenish it if you've spent it). This means once you're done saving, you'll have some free wiggle room in your budget for other goals.

Takeaway actions
- Make sure you have both a checking account and a savings account.
- Don't pay any fees, please. Spend your money on things you care about, not banking.
- Automate your banking so all your bills are paid on time and you don't have to worry about them.
- Start an automatic monthly transfer to start saving for an emergency fund.

Chapter 3: #adulting

Being an adult is the best (all you can drink mimosas at brunch!) and the worst (rush hour traffic on your commute). Here are a few thoughts about #adulting and some tips for making your adult life easier so you can enjoy more mimosas.

Getting organized

It's time for me to be honest. Do I seem like I have my act together? Do I seem like the most organized and fiscally savvy gal you have ever encountered? Oh do go on.

Here is reality: I have been an official adult for more than a decade. Until I was 28 years old, I kept all of my important papers in a bin. This bin:

So embarrassing.

I didn't have a desk, so I just threw everything important into this bin. Checks, blank thank you notecards, my passport, medical documents, my lease, broken pencils, my Social Security card, an old alarm clock, a gazillion paperclips, important mail, pay stubs, used up highlighters, tax information, wrapping paper. It was all in there.

To give myself a little credit: I never lost an important document, so at least I was consistent about tossing crap in there.

However. As I'm sure you understand, the situation was not great. I move a lot. Lugging this bin of unsorted paperwork around with me was not a good use of my energy or the gas I use moving crap around.

Second, the bin went under my bed. It was annoying to go searching under the bed every time a piece of mail came in.

Third, there were multiple panic-filled moments when I spent time rummaging through the bin praying I had actually followed my system. Lots of stress and anxiety and self-scolding for not being a more organized person.

I needed at least an intermediate step...so I did this:

What you are looking at is a beautiful plate with an octopus on it (see the tentacles peeping out of the bottom left?) my aunt and uncle gave me. It became my mail receptacle. And by mail receptacle I mean place to put towers of mail until they got too tall and they fall over and I had to shove them in the bin under the bed.

You can see why this system was not great either. I couldn't even see my pretty plate.

Finally, at the age of 28 and 2 months old, I finally decided to keep my paperwork like a grownup.

I invested in an ugly file folder crate and some hideous green hanging folders. Now when my mail stack gets too high, I file the important paperwork. I don't even keep those little empty mailback envelopes they give you! I get rid of them right away! The files and box weren't cheap, they don't look nice, and it is definitely not my favorite part of being an adult.

However.... after being an adult for over a decade now, having this file box does make me *feel* more like an adult. Plus, I no longer freak out about where my Social Security card is (what is that thing for, anyway?)

The ugly bin. I am such a responsible adult.

So you see, I am not a naturally organized person. I don't have a label maker and I don't want one. The reason I have organized my finances the way I have with automatic bill pay and instant budgeting is because if I didn't have it automated, my bills and important paperwork would have ended up in the under-the-bed-lack-of-filing-system and I would have no clue about my money at all.

You will also notice I didn't come up with this new organization system overnight. I had a few failed experiments including:

- A pink binder that did not have enough space in it and I also couldn't find the hole punch
- Multiple shoe boxes that I moved around with me
- A lovely patterned storage container that got crushed during a move

The point is— sometimes you are going to try to set up a system, and it won't work. You might need to set up a system one piece at a time (the mail plate was a genius step for me to avoid making my roommates crazy with my old bills stacked on the hall table...) But if you keep trying different systems then one day you will find a system that works for you. Then you'll be able to find your Social Security card in a pinch.

Dealing with paperwork

I am a magnet for paperwork problems. I am not kidding. My paperwork issues are out of control. I know I am in trouble when the person I am talking to says, "Huh. That's weird" when looking up my information. Some examples:

- I had to get my diploma printed three times because they kept misspelling my name.
- I sold my car and cancelled my car insurance. I got billed the next month. I called again to cancel. I got billed again. The next month, I was told I needed to send in proof I actually sold my car. I sent in the paperwork. They said it didn't count because it wasn't notarized...as if I had the option to go back in time to get the paperwork notarized. (That thump you just heard was me hitting my head against the wall). It took six months of back and forth before I fixed it.
- I was accepted to a fellowship. Two weeks before the fellowship started I got an email saying I needed to turn in employment paperwork and I needed to have it notarized and it needed to be there the next day. I ran all over town getting the paperwork notarized and arranging for next day delivery. It turned out the paperwork the office had sent me was for 2008 and therefore expired and only valid for the Northern Mariana Islands. I am not joking. Had to do it again.

See what I mean? These are only the examples that didn't take me an hour to type up. I'm sure you have examples like this of your own.

Unfortunately, financial management means lots of paperwork, and whenever there is paperwork there is significant potential for head-thump-inducing problems. All of the examples above would have cost me money (in the case of the incorrect diploma it could have cost me a future job!) and none of them were caused by anything I did. Sadly, this is common— usually someone else's mess-up will cost you your hard-earned cash, and that stinks. Lucky for you, I have learned a few strategies that have helped me cope and recoup my money.

How to deal with customer service

1. **Document your interactions.** Whenever someone promises to do something for you (cancel your car insurance, spell your name right this time) write down their name, their employee ID number, the date you spoke, and exactly what was promised. Sometimes I trust people and I forget to do this, and sometimes it bites me in the butt. If I ever have to make the same call twice, I start taking notes— but my life would be easier if I just did it from the start. This is especially useful dealing with the cable company. I have found cable companies tell you different things every time you call. Keep calling until someone tells you what you want to hear and then write down that person's information and use it to get what you want.

2. **Ask for some role reversal.** The customer service representative you are speaking with (incompetent as he or she may seem) is paid to know more about the company policies than the customers. Ask them to use their expertise and put themselves in your shoes. I usually say, "I know I

am not the first person in the world to have this problem. If you were me, what would you do to solve this problem?" It usually works. Don't be afraid to be pushy (but polite) with this technique. Flatter the incompetent who is helping you and remind them they are the expert in this situation and ask for their expert advice.

3. **You catch more flies with honey than vinegar.** This tip feels like the exact opposite of what you want to do. You are dealing with the world's most incapable person who has ever been given a job and you are getting frustrated. I get it. But you are the only one fighting for you. If you hang up the phone, you still have the problem and no one will fix it. So, take a deep breath and be the nicest version of yourself you have ever been. When my sister was getting married, she was having a terrible time getting a contract from the reception venue and the coordinator was not responding to calls or emails. When she finally was able to schedule a meeting (wedding in five months with no confirmed location), my understandably frustrated and worried sister baked cookies for the coordinator and started the meeting off by thanking the coordinator for her help and support planning the wedding (my sister wasn't even sarcastic— truly an incredible feat). The coordinator produced a contract at the meeting and my sister and her fiancé got a better price than they had been expecting.

Finally, stick with it. Patience is the key to victory. I have a diploma with correct information on it (in my file folder system!) I no longer pay for car insurance for a car I don't own. I am legally employed and not in the Northern Mariana Islands. It might be painful getting there, but be persistent. I have hope that one day I will wake up and notice I haven't had a ridiculous paperwork problem in over a week. A girl can dream, can't she?

Shopping around for services

I don't know about you, but dealing with everything to do with healthcare freaks me out. I don't like making appointments, I don't like talking with doctors, I don't like feeling sick, I don't like going in when I am feeling healthy because the only news you will get is you are not healthy after all. I really don't like (and don't understand) health insurance.

I get especially freaked out about doctors and money because sometimes doctors don't tell you the test they are doing and then six months later you get an outrageous bill. I already feel nervous and intimidated and often I feel like I am being rushed along when I am in the office and I never remember/feel awkward asking about the costs of the procedures.

Needless to say, I am not ready to write about making good financial healthcare choices because it is an area of adulthood I definitely don't excel at.

It is something I need to work on. But I took a baby step towards getting over that by starting with a doctor and a procedure I am very comfortable with— a cleaning at the dentist.

Here is what I did:

I am overdue for a cleaning, but I don't have a dentist in the area. I looked on Yelp to find a highly rated dentist. When I called to make an appointment, I asked (big step for me!) how much a standard new patient cleaning costs. $250! Holy cow! I said thank you and hung up without making an appointment. Not too hard or too embarrassing.

I kept calling around and was quoted prices from $190 to $340 (how is this last dentist even sleeping at night?)

Finally, I found a dentist who has 5 stars on Yelp who charges $150 for a new patient cleaning. Perfect.

Baby steps. Instead of showing up, having my teeth cleaned and then being shocked at the bill, I did a little research and saved myself a bit of anxiety. I also saved myself a potential $190.

I think I'll try this again in the future.

Taxes gross

I think taxes really stink. And it's not because I think taxes shouldn't be paid. I love smooth paved roads! I love having someone come rescue me if my house is on fire!

What I hate about taxes is how freaking hard they are to figure out. I am pretty smart. I can read. I have a dictionary. I have the internet. I have no idea what tax words mean and I am terrified of interpreting them wrong. I got audited one year and it was so embarrassing and terrible (and what a stigma!) I am a good person! Why do I need an audit? Don't they trust me?! (No. They don't. And I did my taxes wrong. So that is why I got audited.)

You know how I am your personal finance guru, with all the answers about everything to do with your money? How I have tens of thousands of admirers around the globe and I have helped a gajillion people get their finances in order? I have been audited (described above. An emotionally traumatic experience). When I started freelance writing and my paychecks didn't have taxes taken out, I knew I had to pay some sort of independent worker tax but I had no idea how much or to whom and I didn't know where the forms were. I knew I would be penalized if I just ignored it (and I hate paying fees!) but I put it off from March to December 27. That is a lot of procrastination. I had no excuse at all, except I was scared of doing something wrong again and embarrassed I didn't know what to do, given my status as an internationally famous financial whiz. And guess what? I just had to google the forms and it was maybe 11 minutes of work. That I had put off for nine months....

So, it's completely normal for you to be scared and embarrassed about not knowing about taxes. Unless it's your job, it's kind of lame to have all the answers about taxes. But we still have to pay them, and this year is a good year to get over your fear! Why? How? Glad you asked.

You can always do your taxes yourself, without any accountant or special software. Your local library will have copies of the forms you have to fill out or you can google and print them (it should be a 1040EZ, 1040A or 1040, depending on your income level). The tax forms have instructions and definitions on them in the tiny writing in the back of the packet, but it's ok to find that intimidating and not want to do it. There are some other options.

-You can hire an accountant or a tax preparation service like H&R Block. This will cost you, but you're paying for their expertise and to not do it on your own.

-You can do it yourself with TurboTax or other similar software. Again, it costs a little, but the software makes it easier on you.

-The IRS has a set of really great volunteers (google "VITA tax preparation") who will help you do your taxes for free if you make $54,000 or less, are disabled or if you are a taxpayer with limited English. You don't have to know all the answers because these lovely people do! I started volunteering as a financial coach with a number of these folks in my state and let me tell you, they are smart and sharp, funny and kind people. They have also seen everything there is to see in terms of rough tax preparation, so you don't have anything to be embarrassed about. You get hand holding during the tax prep process, you get to meet some nice, capable people, and you don't have to live in shame and fear like me.

Taxes are the pits, but you gotta do 'em. Don't extend your tax return deadline if you can help it, because you will pay penalty fees and you know how I feel about those.

Takeaway actions and ideas:

- Being an adult is hard.
- Create an organization system in a way that works for you.
- Advocate for yourself when you come up against paperwork problems.
- Ask how much medical procedures and services cost.
- Go drink a beer.

Chapter 4: Budgets

Budgets sound like they are *no fun*. I am betting even the word budget makes you feel guilty and maybe a little scared. I used to feel exactly the same way. I thought if I had a budget, then I was certainly going to go over that budget every month, and then instead of feeling vaguely guilty about something I didn't really know about I would have a real reason to feel guilty for mismanaging my finances. If I didn't have a plan, I couldn't feel bad about not following the plan, right?

Except that without a plan, how do you know if you can afford to do the things you want to do?

Without a plan, you are much more likely to overspend and get yourself into debt you could have avoided in the first place. I wanted to join a pretty swanky gym when I moved to my neighborhood. I had never joined a gym before because I thought it would be too expensive but because I had a budget, I figured out I could afford the membership (hellooooo sauna!)

Are there things you only do occasionally, like take rideshares instead of buses? How much is it costing you? How do you know, unless you track where your money is going? I don't have a car, and before I had a budget I felt guilty every single time I called a ride instead of waiting for the bus. Every time. But you know what? Now I have budgeted ride money into my monthly plan. I can take as many rides as fit in my budget, and I never have to feel bad about it! Once I have used up my monthly ride budget, then it is bus stopville for me, but until then, I have given myself permission to stop feeling guilty about spending on luxuries because I know I can afford it. It is an amazingly liberating feeling.

Also, I know if I do badly on following my budget one month...well, it is a guide for myself and only for myself. I'm not getting graded. There is always next month, and I can always reassess and adjust my budget as need be.

Budgets sound terrible, but they are really freeing. They free you from guilt. When you budget for everything you have to pay for (stupid electricity bill) and everything you should pay for (emergency fund, retirement) then everything you have left over is yours to do whatever you want with.

Anything at all.

Want to spend the remainder of your budget playing penny slots after flying first class to Vegas on a whim? You are being totally responsible! That is a legitimate way to spend your money because you already took care of all of your responsibilities!

Don't you feel better? Don't you want to make a budget? Aren't budgets fun? Isn't Vegas fun?

Actually making a budget

So you are convinced it is a good idea to make a budget, right? Right! But how do you start? I made you a personality quiz to get things going.

Budget tracker personality quiz

Directions: If the statement applies to you, write down the letters that correspond to the question. Then add up the number of times you get each letter and read about the budgeting technique that will best fit your needs below.

1. I love details: **A, B, C**
2. I like apps: **A, E**
3. I'm super broke: **A, B, C**
4. I hate spending time and energy on my money: **A, D, E**
5. I like looking at patterns: **A, B**
6. I'd be ok only using one credit card: **A, B, D, E**
7. I meet my savings, emergency fund and retirement goals every month: **D, E**
8. I don't want to use a credit card: **B, C, D**
9. I'm super tech savvy: **A, D, E**
10. I like cash: **B, C**
11. I'm certain I live below my means: **D, E**
12. I'm freaked out about computer security and money: **B, C, D**
13. I'm very goal oriented and get motivated when I can track my progress: **A, B, C, E**
14. I'm in credit card debt: **A, B, C, D**

Mostly A's: Automated penny tracking

If you're broke and you're into automation, you can use a personal finance tracking software that links to your credit cards, bank accounts— even your investment accounts. I use Mint, which is very secure (and pretty awesome), but there are other options out there. Mint works by linking all of your accounts into one website so you can look at your spending, your budgets, your savings goals and your investments all in one place. Nice. Mint automatically uploads your spending and files each purchase into your budget tracker, so you can see how you are doing for each category. Mint also tracks long term trends in spending. It's pretty great. Of course there's an app, so you can get alerts on your phone if you're getting close to your budget limit in a category.

Mint isn't the only software out there, so pick one that works for you.

Software tracking doesn't work well with cash and it is a bit of a hassle to get set up, but it's nice to be able to look at trends and patterns over time. If you're broke or working towards paying off debt or saving for a goal, this is a great, low effort way to track your spending and make sure you're on target to meet your goals.

Mostly B's: The worksheet method

Not into apps or sharing your bank info with a third party? Make your own spreadsheet and fill in your expenses or get out the old pen and paper. Pros: You can adjust it to fit your lifestyle. This is good if you have complicated finances or if you mainly use cash, because you will have to manually enter your expenses anyway. Also, you can keep it supersecure by saving it only to your computer or hiding your notepad under your mattress at home. Cons: Pain in the butt. High maintenance, and you really have to be committed. If you're on a tight budget, you have to update this system fairly often. If you suspect this will be too much work for you, don't do it. Make it easy on yourself to stick to a budget!

Mostly C's: The envelope method

You start each month by taking the amount of money you have for variable expenses in cash. Is your budget for groceries, clothes, gas and restaurants $800? Take out exactly $800. Then, divide it up based on your budget categories. I have heard this called "the envelope method" because one way to keep it organized is to carry around a pile of envelopes full of cash with each budget category written on them. You can also buy one of those coupon sorters. Or, you can use paperclips and post-its. Whatever. You pick how to keep it sorted! The point is— if you have spent all of the money in your envelope for groceries, that's it. You can either borrow from another envelope, or you can put some groceries back on the shelf. You're breaking the rules if you use your credit card or take out any more cash (and you're kind of breaking the rules if you move money from one envelope category to another, but whatever. You are your own boss.)

This is very effective if you find you go overboard holiday shopping. Decide before you shop how much money you are going to spend on the holidays in total, and then how much you are going to spend on each person, and then use the envelope method. This is especially useful at the holidays because gifts for other people (that you have to pay for all at the same time) are a budget abnormality, and even a budgeting rock star can lose track. This way you have planned ahead, and you won't have any fiscal regrets in the New Year!

This is also a good strategy because when you pay with cash, you are more aware of how much actual money is leaving your account and cash users spend 20% less than credit card swipers, on average. When you break a $50, that $50 is never coming back to you. If you have a problem with overspending in general, you might think about switching from swiping credit cards to a cash-only scheme.

Mostly D's: The low tech/lazy method

This method only works if you aren't in debt and you know for sure you have a lot of "free" money in your budget. The low tech/lazy method is this: You get a pad and paper. You write down your income. You write down your general expenditures. You subtract the expenditures from the income.

If that number is big, this system is okay for you. Think about your goals and automate some of that "spare" money into a designated account for those goals. Keep an eye on your bank accounts and make sure they aren't shrinking too much. Check in on your notepad estimates every six months or so. That's it! Note that if you don't have a lot of wiggle room in your budget, this will not work for you. Budgeting, like many things in life, is easier if you have money.

The point of this budget is to make sure you're not setting yourself up for failure by overspending or overcommitting to fixed expenses. If you have a big cushion of "free" money, you don't have to track every penny— but how to you know if your cushion is big enough unless you do some basic math?

Mostly E's: Occasional checkup

This method is good if you aren't in debt and you know you have a lot of "free" money in your budget, but you want to make sure you aren't spending like a crazy person in specific categories. For this method, set up a low tech/lazy method (see above) and then put all of your variable expenses on a single credit card. Set up a Mint account that is attached only to that credit card, and then create budget limits just for the categories you are worried about. When I did this, I tracked eating out, groceries and our Amazon prime addiction. I managed to cut each category by about half just by being a little more mindful and aware of our spending habits.

How to use your personally tailored budget management strategy

Step 1: Figure out your income. All budgeting starts in the same place— income. Some people have a fairly steady income and should know how much money is coming in. If you have a variable income, you need to treat it like you treat your spending— use your best guess based on history/upcoming income you know about, and be conservative. Update it as you learn more.

Step 2: Estimate your outflow. After you know how much money hits your bank each month, start by getting an idea of where your money is going now. A baseline, if you will. Use the technique that will work best for you, based on the budget tracker quiz! It will probably take a few months for you to get a full picture of your expenses, but don't let perfection get in the way of planning. Estimate now and then you can adjust as you go. First you need to make a list of the main expenses that come up regularly in your life. Here are examples of categories from my own budget:

- Rent
- Utilities
- Cable/Internet
- Phone
- Public transportation
- Rideshares
- Emergency fund
- Restaurants
- Savings
- Gym/Fitness
- Alcohol/Bars
- Retirement investments
- Groceries
- Clothes
- Charities
- Haircuts/personal care
- Travel

If you own a car, add in:

- Car payments
- Gas
- Car insurance
- Parking or tolls (if applicable)

Step 3: Set goal expenditures for each category. Set target amounts of what you want to spend in each category based on how much you normally spend. Be realistic— don't worry about "trimming the fat" just yet. If you usually spend $250 on groceries, don't suddenly expect your spending to drop to $100 just because you wrote it in the budget. Some items won't come up every month— I don't travel every month, but I plan to fly every three to four months, and that is in my budget.

Note that there are two different types of expenses in your budget: fixed and variable. Fixed expenses are costs you can predict down to the penny each month— you know what rent is, you know what trash pickup costs. Variable expenses are just that— variable. They change depending on your consumption, and this is where you have a lot of wiggle room to cut back if you need to.

Step 4: Crunch some numbers. Now, add it up. Is your budget less than your income? Awesome! You aren't off the hook, but you do have some options.

Is your budget more than your income? Still awesome, because now you know where your money is going and you can make a plan to tweak your spending or earn more so you are living within your means. You are becoming empowered to take charge of your financial life, and that is something to be proud of.

Step 5: Track your spending. So now you know what's coming in and you kind of think you know what's going out. How do you make sure your guesses are accurate and you are on track to meet your goals? That's why you took the budget tracker personality quiz, to figure out which budgeting strategy will work best for you.

Step 6: Tweak your budget. After you've tracked spending for a few months, assess how you're doing. Spending more than you thought in a category or two? That's cool. Now you know! You can either shift some things around in your budget or cut back on your spending in that category. Knowledge is power, my friend.

That was it! Budgeting isn't so bad. It's a guideline for yourself and that's it. If you know where your money is going, you can make sure you're spending it on things that align with your goals. If you mess up, try again next month. Simple as that.

How to decide what you can afford

If you are in your twenties, you are probably making some big life choices. When you move, switch jobs, go to school, get married, have kids — you have to readjust your budget.

No big deal— you already know how to do that! But what if you are about to make a big commitment (signing a lease, buying a car) and you aren't sure if you can afford it?

Let's rewind in my life, back to 2013. I was moving to a new (expensive) city. I had a new income. I had sold my car but I wasn't sure how much I would be spending on public transportation or cabs (how was I supposed to know, I hadn't been there yet!) How much would food be? (turned out my closest grocery by about a half hour walk was Whole Foods...it's not called Whole Paycheck for nothing!) Word on the street was everything was pricier in this city, and I no longer had the luxury of a car to drive to farther, cheaper stores.

When I was house hunting, there was a huge range of rent prices in the areas I could reasonably commute from. Places that looked like dumps to me were $700 for a room with multiple roommates, while nice one bedrooms were about $1900. But what could I afford? I didn't want to sign a lease and then have trouble paying rent, but I also had more income coming in than I had in the past and I felt like I could move a step or two up in the housing world.

The first thing I did was estimate my take home pay. I knew what my total salary was, but it is always a surprise when you see the amount on your first paystub (oh Uncle Sam, you get me every time). If you forget to calculate in taxes, you can be really up a creek. I googled a tax calculator to estimate, and then I subtracted $200 per month just to be safe.

Then (I really did this because I had no idea) I googled how much of your paycheck should be going to rent. The standard response is you should be paying no more than 30% of your take home income in rent. Sounded good to me, and I could move a step or two up from the dump apartments!

Spending 30% of my income on rent meant I ended up in a lovely house with two roommates. Definitely not a dump, but not a luxury one bedroom apartment in the middle of all the action, either. It suited my commuting needs, I was in a safe neighborhood, and I made friends with my roommates. Most important to me, I never had trouble paying the rent.

Even though it turned out many parts of my new city were more expensive than I had planned, I knew my fixed costs (rent) were within my budget. Because I am pretty savvy about reducing my variable costs if I must (food, transportation— even utilities) I was mainly concerned with making sure I could afford my fixed costs. When you're in this situation and you're trying to figure out how big your mortgage payment should be, set up a mock budget and see how much wiggle room you have while still meeting your other financial obligations.

What to do when you win the lottery

...or get your tax refund.

Suddenly you have a ton of money! Yeah! But what do you do with it? You are my wise and clever reader, so you know it is not smart financial planning to blow it all on a sports car. But this new money isn't in your budget, so how do you fit it into your spending and your goals?

First, you celebrate! It's exciting, you have a little spare cash. Go buy that jacket you have been dying for. Try that new restaurant. Replace your ratty old gym clothes with something that makes you excited to exercise. Make the celebration reasonable— it should be about 10-20% of your new cash money. Spending $500 on a new tv when you got a $1000 tax refund might be going overboard, but going on a movie date is a nice splurge.

Next— look at your debts and your savings goals.

- Can you pay off a credit card with this cash? Won't that feel awesome, to not pay interest anymore?
- Have you started your emergency fund? Then you won't have to worry about unexpected expenses.
- Can you invest it in your retirement accounts? Earn some crazy compound interest on this free money to make even more free money?!!
- Should you use it to pay off some student loan debt?

If I were you, I would do a mix of the things above with my newfound cash— but you have to be wise about it (consider your interest rates, my friend). If you can pay all of your debt off— do it! But paying just some of your debt off all in one big chunk may not actually be the best choice.

What if the cash you just received is big for you, but it is just a fraction of your overall debt?

While the mathematically optimal way for you to pay down your debt is to immediately put your windfall towards the large balance you're carrying, this might not be the method that best fits your lifestyle. Do you feel like you're drowning in debt and does it feel like you can't get out from under it? Applying your lottery winnings to your debt as monthly payments for a few months may help relieve some of the pressure and give you some space and time to make a budget and a debt reduction plan. Don't slack off, but instead think of it as a grace period so you can focus on making a plan while you get a mental break from worrying about debt payments.

Takeaway actions and ideas:

- Create a budget. Budgets tell you if you can afford to do the things you want to do and reduce guilt about spending on yourself.
- Six steps to making your budget: 1. Know your income. 2: Estimate expenses. 3: Set goals for your expenses. 4: Crunch some numbers. 5: Track your spending. 6: Adjust course if you need to.
- There are a number of different ways to set up budget tracking; pick the way that works for you.
- If you're trying to decide if you can afford a big purchase, make a mock budget and play around with it.

Chapter 5: Credit

I know you've all seen those commercials telling you to check your credit or you'll be living in your parents' basement, but what exactly is credit? "Credit" generally refers to your credit score, which is a number that grades you on how risky it may be to give you a loan.

Having good credit means you are expected to be a responsible money borrower— you will probably pay your loans back in full and on time. Good credit is often rewarded with the ability to borrow more money and you're usually offered lower interest rates on loans. Bad credit means you are considered a higher risk loan customer. It might be harder for you to get a loan, and your interest rates will probably be higher.

What is a credit score? A credit score is a number between 300 and 850. Seems crappy that all of your brains and beauty and talent should be simplified into one measly number, but that's how life works sometimes. Just like bowling, a higher score is better (do not confuse with golf).

- Below 600 is generally considered not so hot. You might have trouble getting a loan and your interest rates will not be great.
- 600-674 is below average.
- 675-710 is good.
- 710 and above is excellent. You should have no trouble getting a loan and you should be able to get highly competitive interest rates.

A credit score and a credit report are two different things: your credit report provides most of the information that goes into assessing your credit score. They are both important, but the most important task for you is to make sure your credit report is accurate so you have the correct credit score.

When people talk about "identity theft," the big risk is that your credit score will be impacted. Checking your credit report will help you monitor your identity to make sure it is safe. Note: if you are a parent, check your child's credit report too. If there's nothing on there, that's good. If there are credit cards in your six-year-old's name, you either need to have a talk with your kid or you need to report credit card fraud. Also: if you have never taken out a loan or a credit card or had utilities in your name your credit report may also be blank. That's fine, but it's time to start building credit.

How do you find your credit report?

Under law, you can get a free summary of your credit report from each major credit reporting source once a year. There is only one website authorized to give you the official credit report you are legally entitled to. This is www.annualcreditreport.com. They get their data from one of three sources and you can pick one to give you your free report: Equifax, Experian or TransUnion. Any other website has not been federally approved and may be a scam website (and you are putting your Social Security number in there, so be careful!)[*]

Equifax, Experian and TransUnion get their data from different sources, so theoretically your credit reports could be different from each company. You can check your credit report from each of these companies once each year for free. If you are worried about your personal data, you can check all three at the same time; if you'd rather check periodically, you can look at one every four months. I recommend checking your credit report at a minimum of once each year. Set an alert on your phone so you don't forget.

---

[*]Life tip: look for https instead of http at the start of financial web addresses. The "s" stands for "secure." If the website doesn't have an "s," beware!

What is in a credit report?

- Information such as: your address, Social Security number, date of birth.
- How much credit you have access to (loans, credit cards, mortgages etc.) and the dates you opened these accounts. This goes back to when you were 18. The Ann Taylor credit card I signed up for when I bought my first suit? That credit card will be listed on there forever.
- How many loans you have requested. Signing up for lots of credit cards can impact you negatively, which makes sense because if you suddenly take out a loan for a Ferrari, a mortgage on a condo, and open up five new credit cards, you don't seem like such a reliable customer anymore.
- Any outstanding debt or collections you have against you.

If information is not correct on the report, you can file for a correction right on the website. It's relatively easy to do and it's important to maintain an accurate record on your credit report so that you don't have to fix it in a rush while you're applying for a mortgage.

Is my credit score on the report?

Drat! No! You usually have to pay more (between $10 and $15) to get your credit score. If you are thinking about taking out a big loan in the next few years, it is probably worth your money to pay for the credit score so you can factor interest rates into your budget. I get mine every few years just to check in, because there are ways you can improve your credit score if you need to. Free access to credit scores is frequently offered as a benefit to opening accounts at some banks, so check with your bank to see if this is a perk.

What impacts your credit?

There are five different areas that impact your credit score—
check out the table below.

Areas that impact your credit score	
35%	Payment history
30%	Amount owed
15%	Length of credit history
10%	New credit
10%	Types of credit

Payment history

I hope by now you have already automated your bill
payments so you know 35% of your credit score is perfect
because you will never have a late fee!

If you had some errors in the past, those problems may stay
on your report for up to seven years. Sorry. If you are
currently in a dispute over a bill or if you just missed one
payment, make sure you call to ask that the late payment
isn't reported. Usually there is a grace period and you won't
get reported if it has only happened once, so don't freak out.
Also, sometimes (for whatever reason this happens
frequently with medical bills) the first time I get the bill in
the mail it is already overdue. Just pay it as soon as you get it
and save the envelope with the postage date stamp— they
will send you second and third notices before they actually
report you for nonpayment.

A benefit to being young: if you make a lot of credit errors
when you are in your early twenties (we all made a lot of
mistakes when we were in our early twenties, don't worry),
by the time you are ready to buy a house or make a big
purchase, you will probably have moved past the seven-year

mark and your errors will be off your credit report. It is not as easy for a 35-year-old to recover from credit mistakes because a 35-year-old generally needs access to more credit than someone in their early twenties.

Amount owed

The amount owed does not necessarily mean that because you are in debt, you have bad credit. It really refers to a how much you owe compared with how much people would lend you. It's a ratio. If you owe $2,000 on a credit card with a $15,000 limit, you still have $13,000 of credit available. That is good. If you owe $2,000 on a credit card with a limit of $5,000, you only have $3,000 left of credit. That isn't so great. The goal is to keep your debt: credit ratio around 30% or lower.

One way to improve your credit score (immediately! One phone call!) is to ask for a credit increase. This is only appropriate for you to do if you don't have a ton of credit cards and/or loans out, because asking for too much new credit at once can harm your credit report. (Can we never win!?!) But occasionally— maybe once a year, or if you get a raise because they ask about your income— call up your credit card and ask for a credit increase.

Length of credit history

This one is pretty obvious— the longer you have been using credit and paying bills on time, the safer a candidate you are. If you are a freshly minted adult, now is a good time to slowly start using credit to build up a good credit history. Additionally, if you have a credit card you never use but you have had for a long time, don't close that account. Keep it open (a good idea is to put your Netflix subscription on it and automatically pay it off each month, so you don't have to think about it).

Also— closing an account doesn't delete it from your credit history. In fact, it can lower your credit score because of that pesky debt: credit ratio. Sorry, kids.

New credit

If you have suddenly signed up for four credit cards all in the same day (did you get suckered into those 20% off offers at the mall?) then your credit score will suffer, especially if you don't have a long credit history. Any sudden request for multiple forms of credit may lower your score.

This is why I never recommend that people sign up for those store credit cards at the mall. Saving 20% on a pair of sweet shoes may save you $20 today, but a lower credit score can impact your mortgage rates when you buy a house which will cost you thousands of dollars. You should have two or three credit cards, but you should not have a different credit card for every store you have ever shopped in. It is better to have a few credit cards with high credit limits and rewards you can use.

Types of credit

Your score also depends on the different types of credit you have. Credit cards, installment loans, retail accounts, mortgages, car loans are all different types of loans. It's normal for young people to have a credit card and not a mortgage, so don't go buying a house to try to diversify your loan types. It is more important that you are responsible for the types of credit you do have, so when you get older and buy a house you will already have a solid credit score to negotiate with.

A final note about credit scores for all you overachievers— there is no such thing as a "perfect" credit score. You can't get an A+ in credit. Your grandma is always going to have a better score than you because she is older and has been taking out loans and making payments longer than you. Make sure your credit report is accurate, pay your bills on time, and work towards improving your credit ratio. If you do all those things, your score will increase over time so just relax about it!

Credit cards

In a post-recession world, the thought of credit cards and the potential for crippling credit card debt may be scary. It's true that credit cards can get you into a lot of trouble, but they are also one of the best ways for young people to build their credit.

The best way to use a credit card is to pay it off in full every month. This way you won't pay any interest on the things you've bought. If you don't pay it off in full or only pay the minimum payment, you'll be paying interest that averages between 11-25% per year (this is your APR, Annual Percentage Rate).

Owing interest on items you buy with a credit card is like adding an extra fee to the cost of everything you buy. If you charged a $100 pair of jeans and took a year to pay them off on a standard credit card, you'd have paid about $110 for those jeans by the end of the year — and all you have left is a pair of worn out jeans plus you paid $10 extra for them.

You can avoid ever paying any interest on credit cards if you pay in full and on time— this means never charging more than you know you can pay off that month. As always, I recommend automating your bill pay for credit cards so you know you'll never get a late fee charge.

Credit cards are a great tool for young adults to build credit— provided you are responsible about it. Having a credit card also makes shopping online significantly safer than using a debit card— and it's nearly impossible to avoid buying at least some things online. You should never use a debit card for online purchases because that information links directly to your bank and all of your assets; a credit card links to loaned money. If your credit card information is stolen, just call the company, your money will get refunded and you will get a new credit card. This has happened to me a few times and credit card companies are great about being responsive and it has never cost me a dime.

It's smart to have 2-3 different credit cards. More than that can hurt your credit, fewer can leave you up a creek in case your credit card information gets stolen and you have to travel for work tomorrow (not like that has ever happened to me....)

How to pick a credit card

Interest rates

In an ideal world, you will pay off your credit card every month and never pay any interest. Just in case things don't work out that way, there are a range of interest rates credit card companies offer. Some companies offer 0% interest for the first year but rates can go up to 25% APR. Do *not* let 0% interest entice you into a spending spree, because interest will start to be charged at the end of that year, usually at a higher-than-average rate.

There are a few rare situations where you may actually want a credit card with 0% APR. If you have a job that reimburses you for travel or other expenses but is perhaps not as punctual with the reimbursements as you need to pay your bills on time, that is a good time to consider a 0% APR credit card because you know the reimbursement will come through. Just don't be tempted to spend your reimbursement on other things instead of paying off your credit card!

Rewards

I bet you know people who are always flying with rewards points. Credit card rewards can be great, but only if you aren't paying for them by running up credit card debt. If you owe money on your card, forget about rewards and focus instead on paying down your card.

Fee-free credit card rewards are generally earned at the same rates whether you get cash back or travel points. A benefit to a cash back card is flexibility— you can spend your rewards on whatever you want, including travel. A benefit to a travel reward card is it can force you to actually take a dream trip— and then you can brag to all your friends that you took your fabulous vacation using rewards points.

Some credit cards have higher rewards returns, but these usually have an annual fee. Deciding if a fee-based credit card is worth it for you requires a little math:

Option A, paying a fee:
(Average amount you charge each month x 12 x percentage back) - annual fee= your take home benefit

Now, compare it to the fee-free benefits you could earn with another card:

Option B, no fee:
(Average amount you charge each month x 12 x percentage back) = your take home benefit

Which one is bigger? If option A isn't significantly larger than option B, stick with the fee-free option for now. You can also always call the credit card company and ask for a fee waiver, but you will probably have to do this every year and they can always make you pay.

There are often one-time rewards offers when you first sign up for a credit card. Signing up for new credit cards too often can harm your credit, which will cost you more than you could ever make in rewards. If you are signing up for a card you legitimately need, then pay attention to the requirements to earn the rewards— the sign-on bonus rewards are the best rewards you are ever going to be offered.

Hidden benefits of credit cards

Almost all credit cards have little known perks that can save you money in a pinch. These benefits include warranties on electronics purchased with the card, automatic insurance for rental cars, and price protection, which are refunds for purchases entered into the system if the price drops after you made your purchase. You can sometimes get discounts on purchases or gift cards if you purchase them through the credit card website (poke around on your credit card rewards site to see if this applies to you). Though less common, some credit cards offer trip protection or can offer emergency travel assistance. Read the fine print— sometimes using your credit card can save you in a pinch!

Tool for beginners: secured credit cards

If you're brand new to credit cards, if the idea of a credit card makes you feel ill or if you have bad credit and are afraid you'll get into trouble, I recommend you start off with a secured credit card. A secured credit card requires a deposit from you (usually around $200) and then the credit limit (meaning, how much you will be able to charge) should equal that deposit. Once you've used your credit card, you should pay the bill on time— and you won't be able to charge more than $200. If you goof and forget to pay, the credit card company will simply use your deposit to pay what you owe, so you can't get into trouble. If you prove you can pay your bills on time, you will eventually receive your deposit back and then the credit card will be just like a normal credit card.

If you have less-than-stellar credit history, a secured credit card can be a great way to build your credit score back up.

It's especially useful if you have trouble taking out a new card or loan because of bad credit— with secured cards you don't need good credit to open an account.

The one caveat for secured credit cards is they sometimes come with fees or automatic interest. Look for a fee-free and interest-free card from a bank you trust.

Takeaway actions and ideas:

- Check your credit report at least once a year. Check your credit score occasionally, too.
- Pay attention to the five factors that go into your credit score.
- Credit cards can be great for building credit history, but are best used if you pay them off in full every month.
- If you're worried about getting into trouble with a credit card, see if your bank offers secured credit cards.

Chapter 6: Retirement

The concept of having to save a giant pot of money for when you're old is pretty scary when you're 22. Or 32. Or even 42. If you're like me, you start to freak out about how much money you're going to need and how little money you have now. What if you turn out to be the world's oldest living human but you've planned wrong and now you're the world's oldest living broke human, eating gruel with no teeth?

The thing is, the concept of saving for retirement is so anxiety-ridden it often seems easier to do nothing. Which is technically true, but you know what feels better than burying your head in the sand? Feeling like you're getting a really, really good deal.

Every dollar you save for retirement in your 20s, 30s, even 40s is exactly that. A really, really good deal. Here's why: because of compound interest, you're basically getting a sale on dollars for your future. If you start saving at age 20, every $.07 you saved and invested will be worth $1.00 when you're ready to retire. You just got 93% off the cost of your retirement— that's my kind of sale!

Here's how it works:

Compound interest— a modern day miracle!

"Compound interest is the eighth wonder of the world. He who understands it, earns it ... he who doesn't ... pays it."— Albert Einstein

This is my favorite and least favorite topic, depending on whether we are discussing investments or debt. Since we're talking about saving for retirement, this is all going to be in the positive, but remember compound interest works just as effectively against you if it is debt.

Imagine I invest $100 and I get a 10% return each year. The first year, I am going to get $110. That's not really that awesome, but it's not so bad. $10 is better than $0. But then the next year, $110 gets invested instead of $100, and you end up with $121. Your interest starts earning interest. The next year you'll get $133. Within ten years, your $100 will be worth $259. This is because your interest is earning interest which is earning interest. You invested some money and then you let time and compound interest work their magic, and you ended up with over double what you started with.

In case you're not sure investing is the right choice for you, check out this chart that shows what can happen to $1,000:

Number of years	Keep it in your mattress	Keep it in your checking account (0.25% interest)	Keep it in your savings account (0.8% interest)	Invest it at 6%
0	$1,000	$1,000	$1,000	$1,000
20	$1,000	$1,111	$1,233	$3,207
40	$1,000	$1,168	$1,446	$10,285

I hope you can tell by this beautiful table how powerful compound interest is. Compound interest is what allows you to get that 93% discount on retirement. The first time I learned about compound interest, the author said it didn't really matter how much money you invest, as long as you invest something.

I thought, "Well, this guy obviously doesn't understand you have to be rich to invest. If you invest more money at the start you get more money at the end." I felt like I didn't have enough money to start investing and investments are for people who already have money and if that isn't a horrible catch-22 I don't know what is!

But you know what? He was right and I was completely wrong. Because what I had at 25 (ok, what I still have because I am still a spring chicken) is time. If you wait until you are 45 with a higher income to invest, you're at a 60% off sale instead of a 93% off sale— still a good deal, but not as good as it used to be. Even though I expect to make more money and have more to invest at 45, I will never make as much compound interest on the money invested at 45 as I would have at 25.

Examples like this used to piss me off, because I never had $1,000 just sitting in my bank account waiting for me to invest. When I was 24 I was living in a double wide trailer in rural Alabama with two roommates. A big activity for me was driving an hour to go to Walmart. I barely had any income at all, but you know what I did have? $50. And you know what? Compound interest works on $50 too! In 40 years, that $50 from the first year will be worth around $500. Awesome.

In case you don't believe me, here is a visual from my investments.

For four years in my twenties, I invested $50 a month in my retirement account. That is $600 a year— not even a month's rent for me. Four years of investing $600 a year= $2,400 invested. Not a whole lot over four years.

But...please look at the amount of compound interest I have earned. The dark gray line is the amount I initially put in, and the light gray line is the amount I have earned in interest.

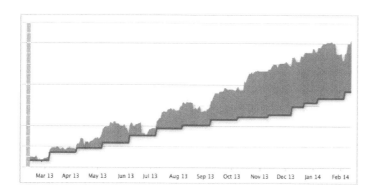

Mar 13   Apr 13   May 13   Jun 13   Jul 13   Aug 13   Sep 13   Oct 13   Nov 13   Dec 13   Jan 14   Feb 14

If you eyeball it, you will notice my investment is worth about a third more than I put in out of my own money. See how the light gray part is growing bigger and bigger and bigger relative to the stair steps? That is compound interest! (The dips are just market variations, I don't worry about those because I don't need this money for a long time). This picture is only showing one year's worth of growth— so imagine what the growth will look like when I retire in 37 years!

Imagine what I could have done if I had started at 18.*

How to get started getting that really, really good deal (aka, saving for retirement)

So saving for retirement is just a fancy way to say you are investing your money and hopefully doing it in a way that keeps you from paying extra taxes. Investing is pretty much the only way to ensure you're earning that sweet, sweet compound interest. Remember that chart you just read when you learned keeping your money in your mattress, a checking account or a savings account wasn't going to pay off in the long run? You need to start earning interest, and you need it now.

---

* Actually, the answer to that the extra $4,200 and seven years would be worth $51,400! Learn from my missed opportunities, all you 18 year olds!

The problem is, investing is super scary and complicated and hard.

Actually, the problem is the people who work on Wall Street want you to think investing is super scary and complicated and hard *so you will pay them to do it for you.* In reality, investing is not scary, it is only as complicated as you want it to be, and it can be pretty easy. It's also way less sexy than it seems. Really successful investing is actually kind of...boring (this coming from the nerdo writing a personal finance book). This is great news for you, because you can successfully invest and save for retirement without spending a lot of energy on your investments or even knowing very much about investing— you can just set it and forget it.

But how do you save for retirement if no one will give you a job with a 401k?

Saving for retirement when you don't have a job that helps you save for retirement

In my early 20s I had some pretty stellar jobs (one year I wrote "shark wrestler" when describing my job to the IRS on my tax forms).

Stellar jobs, yes...but it took until I was 28 to be offered a 401k. I am very aware that saving early will lead to much more wealth in retirement because of the miracle of compound interest. I didn't want to miss out on that extra giant pot of money, but how are you supposed to save for retirement without a job that gives you benefits?

Well, it turns out, you don't need a work sponsored plan to save for retirement. Anyone can save for retirement at any point! A retirement account is really just an investment, and the benefit of a work-sponsored retirement plan is it gives you a tax break on your investments. Even if you think taxes are intimidating and inevitable or if you don't mind paying taxes because you believe in contributing to your community and your country you still want to take advantage of these tax benefits because it's actually better for everyone (country included) if you are financially self-sufficient when you retire. Paying taxes will make this harder, so take advantage of the government programs that offer you tax breaks when you can.

Guess what? You don't need a work sponsored plan to get tax benefits! Check it out:

My favorite financial tool of all time is a Roth IRA. It is named after Senator William Roth, who led the fight to help create this awesome savings tool. IRA stands for Individual Retirement Account.

A Roth IRA is the best choice for twentysomethings.* ** A Roth IRA is a fund that contains your investments (similar to a 401k in this way), but the biggest difference between a Roth IRA and a 401k is the timing for when you pay taxes, and the Roth is a great deal.

There is also something called a traditional IRA, but if you expect to make a ton in compound interest (which you do because time is on your side)— then go for a Roth IRA***.

---

* You can actually open a Roth IRA as soon as you get a job that you file a W-2 for. If you're 15 and working at Dunkin' Donuts, you can open a Roth IRA. If you start saving for retirement at 15 that's like getting a dollar for every nickel you put in (your investment will be 20x as big as what you deposited). And you only ever pay tax on that first nickel. Parents, wunderkinds- take note.
** I said twentysomethings but in reality a Roth IRA is the best choice for everyone unless you are very rich and very old. If that is you, thank you for buying my book, but you aren't really my target audience.
*** A traditional IRA is funded by money that is not taxed

Roth IRAs do have income limits. If you make over $122k individually or $193k as a couple, you can't get a Roth IRA and you should get a traditional IRA instead.

Are you convinced a Roth IRA is an excellent choice? Me too. Here are some things to know:

- In 2019, you can contribute up to $6,000 to your Roth IRA each year. The more you invest at an early age, the better your compound interest will treat you!
- If you are married, both you and your spouse can have a Roth IRA even if you only have one income (which means double the potential for investing!).
- You can always take out the initial contribution you had invested without penalty. This makes the Roth IRA kind of like a secret savings account for yourself— except compound interest is so good I do not recommend you take money out of your Roth IRA except in extreme emergencies and assuming you've already tapped out all your other savings accounts.

If you want to take out any of the interest your money has earned and not just the money you put in, you will pay a 10% penalty if you are not at least 59 ½ years old, unless you are taking it out for any of the following reasons:

- Educational expenses
- Medical expenses over 7.5% of your adjusted gross income
- First time homebuyers can take out up to $10,000
- Costs of a sudden disability

You need to have opened the account at least five years ago before you can access these options. Even if you aren't

---

when you put it in, but when you take the money out you pay normal income tax on what you withdraw.

convinced you're ready to invest, it is worth it to open an account with $5 so you start the clock, because this is an awesome tool to have on hand just in case you need it five years from now.

Even though you still have access to all of this money in case of a big emergency, if you spend your retirement savings early, what will you do when you retire? Also, remember each $1,000 you put in today could be worth over $10,000 when it is time to retire. I don't want to rob my future self of that easy money. I pretend the money is gone and I have promised myself I am not touching it.

How to open a Roth IRA

My good friend Kimberlyn and I were talking about personal finance at a party (I am a really fun party guest). Kimberlyn told me when she was in college she had a professor who told everyone they should open up a Roth IRA immediately. Kimberlyn's response?

"I couldn't even afford crackers, how could I save for retirement?"

I hear ya, Kimberlyn. Not only is it pretty intimidating to open up a new type of money account for the first time, but you were told to do it when you had no money at all. I was super broke in college— it's not an easy time financially, and it is hard to think about saving long term when you are buying store brand saltines.

But Kimberlyn's professor was right, starting a Roth IRA as early as possible will pay off hugely in the long run (because of compound interest. Do I sound like a broken record yet?)

Lots of Roth IRAs have a minimum deposit of $1000-$3000 before you can even open an account. I had never had $1000-$3000 sitting around, and you better believe that my ramen lifestyle was never going to allow me to save up $1000. Luckily, I found an easier way to get started.

At the time, T. Rowe Price had a program that allowed you to start a Roth IRA with $50 a month if you set up automatic deposits. I had $50 a month, I already loved automatic deposits— boom! Roth IRA was set up and my compound interest makes me happy every day! That cashola has grown quite a bit.

After you put some money in, it sits in a "money market fund," which is an investment account without FDIC insurance (remember this is different than a "money market account.") While it's in there, it is not doing much. The money market fund is basically a holding tank for your retirement— you still have to actually move your money into investment accounts with some earning potential.

Here is where I started to get scared. I knew nothing about the stock market. I didn't want to learn what the symbols and the new words meant. I had $50 and was working 80 hours a week without reliable internet access and the nearest library was an hour away. I didn't have time or the money to muck around with trading stocks and paying fees ("um, I would like to buy 1 share of stock X for $14. Oh, the trading fee is $6 per transaction? Huh.") and mainly I didn't want to sound stupid while I was asking for help, so I chose to put all of my money into the 2050 targeted index retirement fund and I *let it sit*.

A targeted index fund is a diversified set of investments. Diversified investments are a mix of higher risk but potentially higher earning investments plus some lower risk and probably lower earning investments—and some middle risk and middle earning investments. Diversifying is a good investment strategy. The idea behind diversifying is that you win some and you lose some, but you generally see growth as the economy grows and you minimize your losses because you didn't invest all of your money in one area that might not do as well.

An index fund is a combination of different investments all bundled together (called an "index"). An index fund's goal isn't to "beat the market" but instead to mirror the performance of the average of a section of the stock market. This sounds not that great because you're shooting for average, but it's actually fantastic.

First of all, it's mathematically impossible for everyone to beat the average, and if you're interested in that strategy you're probably paying someone a lot of money to manage your investments.

Second, the way the economy works is that it usually grows over time. This means that if you keep up with the average economic growth in an index fund, your investments should also grow over time (and you don't have to pay anyone exorbitant fees to manage your money for you).

So basically, an index fund is a diversified way to earn the average amount people earn by investing. Fine by me, I couldn't afford to play any high-risk or complicated games.

The "targeted" part of a targeted index fund means that there is a set end date when I want to start pulling my money out. This investment will become more and more conservative automatically as I get closer to when I want to retire and will need the money— it automatically lowers the chance that I will lose everything before I want to retire. In my case, I will be 65 in 2050 and that's why I picked the 2050 fund. You should choose the one that is closest to your retirement age.

Index funds are the least sexy, most effective ways to save for retirement. They have slow and steady growth and relatively low costs. Actively managing your investments can cost a lot in transaction fees and there have been multiple studies that show that even the most successful fund managers are really just lucky guessers (guess what! They usually come out...average. Exactly where your index fund puts you!) — plus you actually won't be able to manually diversify as much as an index fund does. The best bet for you right now (and honestly for the long term as well) is the boring, safe, diversified, optimized, targeted index fund.

The bad news: T. Rowe Price doesn't offer the awesome $50/month sign up deal anymore...so you guys can't copy what I did exactly.

The good news: Many banks offer this same deal. Just google.

Look for an investment account that has no minimum and no annual fees. You can still set up automatic $50 (or $5...whatever you can afford) deposits, so you can do exactly what I did.

One thing to pay attention to before you choose an investment firm is the expense ratio— this will be associated with the fund you pick. An expense ratio is an amount your investment firm charges for managing your investments. Expense ratios are usually between .5% and 1%, which seems like not a huge amount, but it adds up. A high expense ratio can mean the difference of thousands of dollars (or tens or even hundreds of thousands) over the course of your career, so *pay attention to expense ratios*!

Side note: most investment firms are making money for "the man." Vanguard is client-owned, so any profits they earn go back to the clients in the form of lower expense ratios and fees. I am a huge fan of Vanguard's business model, but they do require a $1000 minimum investment to open a Roth IRA. If you don't have that amount on hand now, you don't have to wait. Open your Roth IRA with another firm and then roll over (aka "move"— see what I mean? The language is fancy but it's not that hard) your investments into a new

Roth IRA with Vanguard or any other company you think fits your needs. Note: when you roll over, make sure your old investment firm transfers your money directly to your new investment firm and you do not withdraw the money into a personal account— if you do, you will get taxed and possibly pay penalties. Transferring the money directly, investment firm to investment firm, is important, but it's not hard. When you move your money to a new investment firm, the new investment firm will be happy to help make all the arrangements.

Got $50? (or $20?) It is worth it to give investing a whirl because, however old you are, *right now* you can get the best sale on retirement money. You'll never get as good a deal again!

Start with an amount you won't miss. I like to think of the money I invest as "night out equivalents." If I went out for dinner and to a movie once a month, that would cost me about $50. I think it is snugglier (and cheaper) to make homemade or frozen pizza, buy a six pack, and rent a movie to watch on the couch. Look at that! I saved for retirement!

Remember, unlike savings accounts, your retirement investments are not risk-free. However, you will not see your money benefit from compound interest if you don't take at least some risk with it, and it is nearly impossible for the average Joe to retire if he has not invested his cash.

There you go! How to open a Roth IRA (relatively) painlessly. It will pay off big time when you are ready to retire, so it is worth it to get started now!

The 401k…aka FREE MONEY (Or, the 403b if you work for a nonprofit)

"I would never sign up for a 401k because there is no way I can run that far."— my hilarious husband

Back in the day, almost all companies provided their employees with a pension. This meant that after they retired, the retirees would get a certain percentage of their former salary (usually 50%) every year until they kicked the bucket. As you can imagine, a pension is a pretty desirable thing to have because you never have to worry about running out of money!

But then. People started living longer. Which meant it was costing companies a lot more to provide pensions to their employees. Nowadays it is extremely hard to find a job that will give you a pension (except for military, firefighters and police officers and a few other jobs). If you have a pension coming to you, you are the retirement winner. Don't quit your job.

Most of the rest of us who get retirement benefits from their employer have a 401k or a 403b*. The name 401k comes from a tax code, which is boring and kind of confusing (my husband is still lacing up his running shoes), so I refer to a 401k as what it really is and that is *free money* (well, it's a little more complicated but there is free money involved, so let's just call it that for now).

401ks are meant as an alternative to pensions to help you save for retirement. They are investment plans that usually

---

* 401ks and 403bs are basically the same except 403bs are for nonprofits and have lower administrative costs. All of the information in this section applies the same way to a 401k and a 403b, but I can't make my husband's joke work with a 403b.

include a broad portfolio of investments including stocks, bonds and money market investments. You can also choose a targeted index fund for your 401k! Here are a few basic pieces of info about 401ks:

- 401ks are called free money (by me) because when you invest in a 401k, most companies will match your contribution up to a certain percentage of your income (usually 3%). So, if you make $100,000 a year and you invest $3,000 per year in your 401k, your company will also put $3,000 into your retirement. That means you now have $6,000 in your retirement (but you only paid for $3,000). Your company is really paying you $103,000 per year instead of $100,000 (you just got a raise even though you can't access it yet!) This is why it is called free money. Because it is money. That is free. You don't have to do anything except sign up for it (which you should do immediately).
- 401k has an added benefit for those of us who love automation: your contribution to your 401k is paid for with pretax dollars and it is automatic. You never get the money in your bank account so you will never be tempted to spend it.
- You can usually contribute more than your company's match (this is recommended unless you are drowning in debt or you have super tight finances).
- You usually don't actually own the matched money until you have worked for your company for a certain number of years. This is called being <u>vested</u> because it's like your company in<u>vested</u> in you!

If you are paying off high interest debt (like credit card debt), deciding whether to contribute to a 401k or to pay down your debt can be tricky. You should still be putting in enough to take full advantage of your company's match policy (it's like earning 100% plus some extra interest on your 401k! That is a much better rate than whatever your credit card is charging you.) You may want to hold off on investing more than the matched amount until your debt is managed.

Your 401k is earning compound interest, my favorite thing in the world. This means not only are you doubling your investment right away (amazing!) but also, given a little time, your doubled money will start earning interest on its interest (ooh, aaah!). See how it can add up?

Remember the example I gave about investing $1,000 for 40 years at 6% interest? Here is what happens to that $1,000 if the initial investment was matched by an employer:

Number of years	Take your income home and keep it in your mattress	Invest it at 6% on your own	Invest it at 6% with your employer's matching program
0	$1,000	$1,000	$2,000
20	$1,000	$3,207	$6,414
40	It's never gonna grow, guys. Still $1,000.	$10,285	$20,571

Each strategy still costs you $1,000, but now you can expect to get double the return you would have gotten without your employer's contribution! Lovely.

When you first start your job, or, if you already started your job, go to HR and tell them you want to contribute enough to get your full match *immediately*. Stop wasting your free money.

401ks can get complicated. This is because the rules are written by lawyers who want you to be intimidated by the confusing language and complicated (boring) paperwork. It is in the company's best interest to provide you with access to 401k because that is an incentive for you to come work for them...but they hope you don't take full advantage of it because then they have to give you free money. So, the language is confusing, but your company will have a 401k administrator whose job it is to help you with that language. Make friends with your administrator.

Also, there are lots of rules about when you can access your free money (not till retirement unless you want to pay steep fees). There is also a federal limit on how much you can contribute each year to your 401k (in 2018 it was $18,000). There are different contribution rules if you are over 50. Because you put the money in without paying taxes on it, Uncle Sam will take taxes out of your withdrawal from your 401k when you retire. If you take the money out before retirement age you will pay taxes plus a 10% penalty. Boogers. Try to avoid that.

Here is the takeaway: 401ks give you free money. No other way of saving will give you free money right off the bat. So, (if you haven't already) take a deep breath and put on your big-kid panties to prepare yourself for dealing with some complicated rules, call your company's 401k administrator to get your free money, make the full contribution that will be matched, and get ready for retirement on your own tropical island.

The difference between Roth IRAs and 401ks: taxes

Roth IRAs and 401ks/403bs are two different tax incentivized ways to save for retirement— this means, you get a tax break. You might not understand taxes (I don't) but whenever the government lets you save on taxes, do it. It will mean tens or hundreds of thousands of dollars extra in your retirement. Before you invest in the market, make sure you have maxed out all tax incentivized investment options. Here are the choices Uncle Sam gives you:

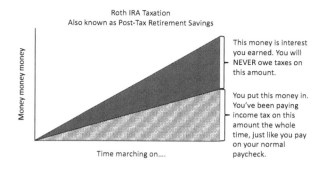

Roth IRA Taxation
Also known as Post-Tax Retirement Savings

This money is interest you earned. You will NEVER owe taxes on this amount.

You put this money in. You've been paying income tax on this amount the whole time, just like you pay on your normal paycheck.

Time marching on....

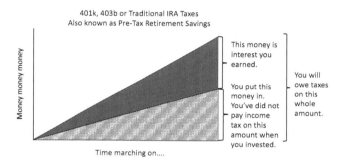

401k, 403b or Traditional IRA Taxes
Also known as Pre-Tax Retirement Savings

This money is interest you earned.

You put this money in. You've did not pay income tax on this amount when you invested.

You will owe taxes on this whole amount.

Time marching on....

You can see when you hit retirement age, you're going to owe more taxes if you have a 401k than a Roth IRA. Here's how you should prioritize your retirement savings:

1. Get the full match from your work's 401k*.
2. Open a personal Roth IRA and max that out.
3. Max out the rest of the 401k.

---

* If your work offers a traditional 401k and a Roth election 401k, I think the Roth is the better choice. This is an area of disagreement that gets really boring about anticipating your tax brackets but here is my opinion: you don't know the future, so why sign up to owe a tax bill when you can pay it off now and earn a ton of tax-free interest.

4. If you still have spare money for retirement (wow, go you), you can invest this normally but there aren't any more tax breaks for retirement accounts.

Don't forget to name a beneficiary (the person who benefits in case you die early in a freak accident). Otherwise the money gets torn up into little pieces and flushed down the toilet. I'm serious. (Just kidding. I'm not serious. It goes to your surviving spouse or next of kin but without naming a beneficiary it's a ton of paperwork and hassle and potential family fighting.) You can name me as your beneficiary, if you want.

If your company goes belly-up before you retire, never fear! Your 401k is safe.* Just take the money and roll it over into an Individual Retirement Account (IRA) so you don't have to pay the 10% withdrawal fee. Mightn't I recommend you roll it over into a Roth IRA?

Takeaway actions and ideas:

- Saving for retirement now is like getting in on the best sale ever, even if you can't afford to save much.
- You can save for retirement on your own and get great tax savings by opening a Roth IRA.
- You don't have to know what you're doing to invest wisely. This is what index funds are for.
- If you're offered a 401(k) or a 403(b), for the love of all things holy get your full match from your employer.

----

*Never fear if you followed my advice to diversify. If you invested your entire 401k in your company's stock and your company went bankrupt, I can't help you. Don't put all your eggs in one basket!

- Taxes are confusing but you should have your retirement accounts in an IRA or a 401(k) or a 403(b). Don't just invest and ignore the tax breaks.
- You have officially made it over one of the hardest financial hurdles that exists. Congratulations!

Chapter 7: Debt

Debt. Do you have any? How do you feel about it? Probably not so great. Maybe it's keeping you up at night. Maybe you want to skip over this chapter because it's too stressful and you just had some major success planning for retirement and you aren't interested in examining your weaknesses, thankyouverymuch.

Debt sucks, I know. But not dealing with debt means next month and the month after and the months after that are going to suck even worse. So let's figure out how to stop the suck and make a plan to get your debt under control. It's ok to hate this chapter, so go get yourself a snack and a nice drink and maybe read this section in a bubble bath.

I'll give you the spoiler up front: Once you implement the recommendations in this chapter, you can stop worrying about your debt. You will make a plan, you can follow the plan. It's going to work, and you will be able to stop worrying.

Kinds of debt

Traditionally people categorized debt as "good" debt and "bad" debt. The basic idea behind these categories is "good" debt is more like an investment that will pay off and in the long run be worth more than you paid (think student loans, buying a house), while "bad" debt is money that you owe for things that are worth less than what you paid for them (think designer handbags and that 2014 cruise).

This good debt/bad debt idea was popular before 2008, when houses were usually worth more than what you paid for them and when student debt wasn't crippling basically every single person in their twenties and thirties. I prefer my new categories of debt, which are "smart" debt and "that was a bad idea" debt.

Smart debt is like the old category of good debt, but it should come with a well-thought-out plan. Education is one of the best ways to get ahead in life, but not all degrees are worth going into debt for. If you've done your research and figured out how much debt you are willing to take on based on the expected gains your new degree will earn you (see chapter 10), taking out a student loan is smart.

Similarly, taking out a reasonable car loan so you can get to work and progress your career is smart debt. Buying a house you can afford in the neighborhood you want to live in long term is smart debt. The theme of smart debt is:

a. You think you can afford to pay it off within a reasonable amount of time
b. The debt allows you to move forward in your life
c. The debt comes with a long term plan

I'm cool with smart debt. Borrowing money is a way to reach your goals, and even though debt is generally icky, smart debt is the best kind. If you're thinking about borrowing money for something and you can't say yes to all three of those requirements, it's not smart debt and that means it's probably not a good idea.

Do we have to talk about the other kind? Nope. Not really. But in exchange for not making you read about "that was a bad idea" debt, you have to go back and read Chapter 4 if you skipped it, and if you owe debt, you have to finish this chapter. It's ok, you have a snack and a beverage and a nice bubble bath to get you through.

Credit card debt

"You want 21% risk free? Pay off your credit cards."—
Andrew Tobias

Did you know, I hate paying for other people to use and manage my money? I hate bank fees, I hate late fees, I hate paying compound interest on my debt.

A pretty crappy deal on taking out a loan is the interest rate you pay on credit cards (didn't think of credit cards as a loan? Well, that's exactly what they are). One of my cards is 17% interest! That means if I have $1000 worth of debt and I only pay off the minimum it will take me five years to pay that debt off and it will cost me $1486! I end up paying almost 50% more for everything I bought with my credit card— not savvy at all. You're paying for designer and you're wearing five-year-old TJ Maxx.

Not only is owing money on your credit cards immediately bad for your closet and your wallet, but as a consumer you should think about where you want your money to go. You have to buy clothes and food and housing, and you have the option to spend your money on other things. You can buy yourself more shoes, donate to charity, buy organic food, buy video games, save for laser eye surgery, give your money to your sister, buy some new wallpaper. That's awesome— you get to choose where your money goes and you can invest in yourself, others, or in something you believe in. If you are spending your money on credit card debt, you are spending your money on supporting credit card companies. These are companies that exploit the part of human nature that loves immediate gratification. Yuck. That is not where I would choose to put my money. I'd rather have a nice dinner out.

Stop a minute. How are you feeling? If you have any credit card debt, you probably feel guilty and annoyed I am telling you how horrible something you already hate is. Completely valid feelings. The real way the economy works is it takes advantage of a few flaws in human nature, and it rewards people who can thwart those instincts with their massive brainpower (this is you, you're obviously a genius if you are reading this book).

The reason why credit card debt is so common is because of something called future discounting (sounds fancy but bear with me). Future discounting is human nature. It means you place less value on $110 you will get in the future than $100 in your pocket today. You can spend that $100 today, but what is that $110 in the future going to get you? You will probably have way more money in the future because you're going be super successful at your dream job that is right around the corner, and maybe that $110 will not buy as much because of inflation, so you would rather have $100 right now.

Credit cards say, "I will lend you $100 right now but you have to pay me back $110 in the future. But remember how in the future you will have sooooooooo much money and the $110 won't even matter to you because you'll have no money worries at all? Doooooo it." So you do. Because you place more value on the money you have today than the unknown future. This is human nature and everyone does it.

This is how credit cards work. Foiled by our own future discounting!

How do you overcome this teeny flaw in human nature to become the master of your own destiny? Here is the strategy:

1. Stop using credit cards to charge more than you can afford. Look at your budget. Is what you are charging in the budget? Will you have enough in your checking account to cover this purchase by the end of the month? No? Then don't buy it.

2. Pay off more than the minimum amount due and set up automatic bill pay. You'll never get a late fee and you won't tempt yourself to just pay the minimum when you pay your bills. If I made $50 payments instead of $25 payments on my TJ Maxx debt, I would pay off my debt in two years and it would only cost me $1,184 total— I could have saved $302 just by paying a little more off each month! Stopping compound debt in its tracks feels just as good as earning compound interest. The end of this chapter has some directions for how to set up your debt repayment plans, so stay tuned.

3. Think about interest rates. If you are investing and earning 6% and you are paying off debt that is costing you 17%, you should be putting that investment money towards your debt. You will save more money by paying off debt than you would make investing. If you have any wiggle room in your budget and if you are putting money into long term savings or retirement (but not money that is getting matched), I recommend you shift that money over to debt reduction provided the interest rate on your debt is higher than the interest rate on your savings.

4. If you haven't maxed out your credit cards and you still have access to some funds in a pinch, it is better to wait before building an emergency fund. If an emergency does happen before you have an emergency fund, you will probably put the expense on your credit card where you will be charged interest— but only if an emergency happens. If you build an emergency fund while paying off your credit card debt, you will definitely pay that interest on your debt. Go with the option where you *might* pay interest rather than the option where you *will* pay interest. This strategy is for credit card debt or other high interest debt only— if you're paying off your student loans, you should still be building an emergency fund.

5. Call your credit card companies. See if they can lower your interest rates, and while you're at it, see if they can stop

charging you any stinkin' fees you might be paying. If you are stonewalled, ask the customer service rep what they would do if they were in your position.

6. If you are still drowning, think about consolidating your credit card debt. To do this, you can transfer your debt to a card with zero interest for a certain amount of time. There are a few pitfalls to this strategy, because opening more credit cards is not necessarily good for your credit and sometimes you have to pay a fee to consolidate. If you choose to do this look for the lowest interest rate. That being said, don't charge more just because you have an amazing (or no!) interest rate for a certain period of time. It will bite you in the butt and then you will have to start over at step 1.

Note: there are organizations that will consolidate your debt for you. Some of these are nonprofit. Some of these are horrible giant predatory scams that will leave you worse off than you started. Even the nonprofits may charge a fee or require that you close your credit card accounts, which may not actually be a good choice for you. You are smart, you're reading my book! You can do this on your own, but if you do need help, make sure you choose an accredited nonprofit and not a scam agency. Look for National Foundation for Credit Counseling accreditation to avoid scammers.

7. Make a plan and stick to it! If you have promised yourself to pay off your newly consolidated debts, that should be your main financial goal. If you are having a hard time laying off the plastic, switch to a cash-only budget. I just read a study that found spending is reduced by 20% on average when you use cash instead of credit cards.

Putting all this into action

So you read this chapter and you think I'm right, but you'd like me to give you some very specific strategies about how to tackle your debt? Lucky you, I've got you covered.

Step 1. Stop borrowing money. No more charging anything on your credit card. No new cars. No payday loans.

Step 2. Tally up the numbers. Go digging under your bed and pull out all your loan documents and credit card statements. Find out who you owe, how much you owe, what you're paying in interest, and what the minimum payments are.

Step 3. Make a spreadsheet or a notepad with those four categories plus a bonus category, "Amount I will pay each month." It'll look like this:

Who do I owe?	How much do I owe?	Interest rate?	Minimum payment	Amount I will pay each month
Totals				

Step 4. Think about yourself. Would you prefer to know you're spending every penny the best way it can possibly be spent even if it might feel like you're not making progress (let's call you a "savvy spender"), or will you do better if you feel like you are overcoming hurdles (let's call you a "motivation maven")? Pick one.

Step 5. Make a plan to fill out the "Amount I will pay each month" column.

Figure out how much you can afford to put towards your debt each month. This should be more than the total minimum amount due and should also be more than the total amount you are paying in interest each month. If you can't afford more than the minimum amount due/interest accruing, you need to slenderize your spending and/or bring in more income (see chapter 8).

If you are a "savvy spender," here's what you do: pay the minimum on all your accounts. Take any money you have left over and put it towards paying off the account with <u>the highest interest rate</u>. Once that is paid off (don't lower the amount you're putting towards your debt!) then move all that money on to the debt with the next highest interest rate. This is the fastest way to pay off your debt and will insure you pay the lowest possible amount of interest as you become debt free.

If you are a "motivation maven," here's what you do: pay the minimum on all your accounts. Take any money you have left over and put it towards paying the account with <u>the smallest total owed</u>. Once that is paid off (don't lower the amount you're putting towards your debt!) then move all that money on to the next smallest total. This way you will get to completely cross bills off your spreadsheet, and it will feel like you are making progress sooner.

The key to success for both of these plans is never to lower the total amount per month you spend to pay off your debt, regardless of whether or not you've paid off multiple accounts. If you were paying $600 a month and now no longer owe on one of your credit cards, don't lower your payments to $500 a month. Maintain pressure!

Let's look at these two strategies after two years of repayment, assuming both Savvy Spender Susie and Motivation Maven Martha have $1,200 to spend on their debt each month:

Who do they owe?	How much did they owe?	Interest rate?	Amount Susie owes after two years	Amount Susie has paid in interest after two years	Amount Martha owes after two years	Amount Martha has paid in interest after two years
Credit card #1	$4,000	14%	$224	$526	**Paid off in 7 months**	$94
Credit card #2	$7,150	19%	**Paid off in 20 months**	$1,231	$3,762	$2,395
Car loan	$9,000	4%	$4,803	$603	$4,803	$603
Student loan #1	$15,000	6%	$6,734	$1,334	$6,734	$1,334
Student loan #2	$6,000	5%	$2,851	$452	**Paid off in 19 months**	$300
Total	**$37,550**		**$14,612**	**$4,146**	**$15,299**	**$4,726**

You can see Susie owes about $700 less than Martha and has paid less in interest, but Martha has already completely paid off two of her bills.

Choose whichever strategy works for you. A plan only works if you will follow it.

Step 6. Automate your repayment plan.

Step 7. Stop worrying about your debt. You made a plan, you're following the plan. It's going to work, so you can stop worrying now!

You might be finding this completely intimidating. You might feel like it is hopeless and you will be mired in debt forever. *You will be fine.* Just like saving up for an emergency fund, eliminating your debt is a slow process. Cut back on your spending, automate your bill payments, and relax about it for now. You have a plan, you are following the plan, and you've automated your plan— and you are right on track. Pay attention to your debt, but stop worrying about it. Check back in in 3-4 months. See how your progress is. Readjust if you need to. When you make a plan for yourself and you follow that plan, you are making the best financial decision you can make. Instead of worrying about unknown debt you can now say with confidence you are in control of your finances and there is no need to worry about the unknown. Do you feel better? Me too.

Outsmarting your student loans

Woohooo you graduated! Things are great! You have that coveted degree (or two) and you never have to take an exam again! Yeah!

Just one thing though...you still have to pay for that degree. For new graduates this can be daunting. Honestly, when I graduated I wasn't even sure how much I owed and who I owed money to. When I first calculated my loan repayment amounts I had to pour myself a stiff drink for the shock...yikes. The number was pretty high— almost as much as my rent! That was with scholarships, working multiple jobs, eating lots of beans and living a very slenderized lifestyle. It's not easy being edumacated, that's for sure.

The first step to handling your student loans: get your bearings

If you're like me, you shoved your student loan paperwork into a bin and then shoved the bin under the bed. I didn't know who I owed money to, I didn't know how much I owed, and I didn't know the interest rates or fees. Luckily, if you owe people money...they will find you and you will soon learn these things, even if you didn't use your careful filing system of shoving the paperwork under your bed.

There are two types of student loans: federal loans and private loans. If you owe federal loans, you owe money to the Department of Education, or if it is a Perkins loan, you owe your school. If you owe private loans, you owe the lender. Here are some things you should know about repaying each of these types of loans:

Federal loans	Private loans
Unless you die, you aren't getting out of paying these off.[*] Bankruptcy does nothing for you.	You might have a variable interest rate, which means what once seemed like a great deal is costing you more and more over time.
Interest rates are fixed and everyone who took out a loan when you did got the same rate, regardless of your credit.	If you had a cosigner who has financial trouble or dies, your loan can automatically go into default even if you've never missed a payment. This will hurt your credit.
You (and your cosigners if you had any) are the only people responsible for this loan. If you get married, your spouse will not have to pay this loan as long as you don't refinance (refinancing means moving your debt to another lender with better interest rates).	There aren't any income based repayment plans or loan forgiveness plans unless you miraculously manage to negotiate for them.

---

[*] Also, if you die, federal loans actually are forgiven, unlike private loans which will cut into your funeral party fund.

You can sometimes figure out an income-based repayment plan that makes it easier for you to pay your bills each month.	If you get married, your new bride or groom is on the hook to pay for your loans if you croak.

If you have private loans, you're pretty much stuck with repaying your loans the way the lender wants you to. You can try to refinance if you can find a better interest rate, but pay attention to fees and whether the interest rates are fixed or variable.

For federal loans, there are a number of repayment plans that are a little more forgiving than the evenly-spaced-repayment-over-ten-years plan. These alternative plans have encouraging titles, such as "Pay as You Earn," and "Income Based Repayment," and they will make paying back your loans a lot more tolerable (at least at first, while you are still working internships while waiting tables on the side). By signing up for one (the paperwork takes a few months, so be prepared) I expect to reduce my required payments by about 75% each month. If you've signed up for one of these income-based repayment plans, you have to file updated financial paperwork each year.

You can be strategic about this! When I entered repayment after graduate school I happened to file the paperwork during the three weeks between graduate school and before I had a job offer. I reported my current income as $0 (which was completely, honestly true because I didn't have a job for those three weeks) and as a result my required payments for the year was $0. I called to check if I needed to update when I got my job, but I was told you only update every year, so I was off the hook for payments for a whole year!

When I refiled the next year, my payments went up according to my new income, but it was very nice for a year to be able to wiggle around with my budget while I moved and set up an emergency fund. I still made it a priority to pay what I could afford each month, but it was nice to have flexibility.

Paying any more than the minimum (even if it's just $50 more each month) will save you quite a bit in interest in the long run. The more aggressively you pay back your loans, the less you will pay in interest and the sooner you can move on with your life.

Speaking of interest— if you can afford to pay more than the minimum, all of your extra payments should go towards the loans with the highest interest rates.

Here are a few tricks that will lessen the total cost of your loans and will not burden you one bit:

- Paying off your student loan interest is tax deductible. Depending on your tax situation, it might be smarter to pay off the interest on all your loans instead of paying down the principal balance so that you can get higher tax breaks.
- Federal loan servicers often offer a slight (0.25%) discount on interest if you sign up to have your loan payments taken directly from your bank account. It is automated (yay! No worries and no late payments!) and a 0.25% reduction in interest on a 10-year, $50,000 loan comes out to be nearly $1,000. I'd like a spare $1,000, would you?
- Consider making your loan payments biweekly instead of monthly (this is especially good if you get paid every two weeks). This way you sneak in an extra month's worth of payments without even noticing the difference in your paycheck. Suppose you pay $500 each month. $500 x 12 monthly payments= $6,000...versus $250 x 26 biweekly

payments = $6,500. On a 10-year $50,000 loan at 7% you will pay your loans off in 9 years and save $2,100 in interest. You never even noticed the difference.

Boom. I just saved you $3,100 and a year's worth of making payments (and maybe some money in taxes!)

Car title loans and payday loans: the worst, most evil money grubbing things ever invented

Both car title loans and payday loans are terrible, predatory traps with super high interest rates that are disguised so you won't think they are that bad. Payday loans, for example, will charge a "fee" that is due within a week or two. If you don't make your repayment, you will owe what you borrowed and a late fee, plus another fee so you can borrow the money again. This seems reasonable, right? Because you're borrowing money and that isn't free.

Except. Credit cards, car loans, mortgages, student loans, personal loans— basically all legitimate loans— share their costs with you as an interest rate— an APR (annual percentage rate) or an APY (annual percentage yield). They don't charge a "fee" per amount borrowed, and APRs are calculated per year, not per week.

A payday loan will charge something like a $10 fee for borrowing $100 for two weeks. That is a 260% APR! (That is not a typo. For reference, the average credit card APR is 16%). If you can't pay off your first loan and need to extend for two more weeks, now you're paying 390%. This only gets worse. In fact, payday loans can charge up to 2100% APR.

Car title loans are similar— they charge a monthly percentage fee, which translates into a huge APR. A 25% monthly fee translates into a 300% APR—and traditional car loans usually have an APR somewhere around 4%!

If you have a car title loan or a payday loan outstanding, do everything (and I mean *everything* short of breaking the law) you can to pay it off. Tap into your retirement funds,* sell your grandma's china, go sell water on the corner. Pay it off immediately if you can, but don't be surprised if they try to claim you can't pay it off ahead of schedule. Expect there to be more fees. Payday loans and car title loans are traps and there is very little oversight of the industry.

Once you pay it off, never take out a payday or car title loan ever again.

A somewhat risky but mathematically sound approach to paying off loans

Have a relative with some spare cash? If you are responsible, have a steady income and have a good relationship with this family member, consider offering them the following: they pay your loans off up front and you repay the family member at a lower interest rate than the lender would have charged you. If you were paying 8% on your loans before, offer your relative 5% interest. Set up a formal agreement with a payment plan (loan calculators are just a google away). If you have proven yourself to be responsible, this could be a win-win: you get a lower interest rate on your loan, your family member gets a 5% return on their investment. Mixing money and relationships with loved ones has ruined many wonderful relationships, so think very carefully before you consider this option.

Takeaway actions and ideas:

• Debt is stressful but being in debt is a fixable situation.

---

* I will never recommend this ever again anywhere in this book so you know I'm serious about paying these loans off.

- There are some benefits to having a credit card and some techniques for avoiding going into credit card debt.
- Don't ever take out a payday loan or a car title loan. Just don't.
- There are a few different techniques to tackle debt— choose the method that will work for you, make a plan, then stick to it.

Chapter 8: When times are tight

I am sorry to tell you there will be times in your life when you just aren't going to have enough money to live a carefree lifestyle. This might be because you've lost your job, gone back to school, had a major lifestyle change (twins?), are buckling down on getting rid of debt, or are getting serious about saving for retirement.

There are three ways to deal with not having enough money: you can spend less, you can earn more, or you can go into debt. Going into debt is not really a manageable strategy long term, so let's discuss the other two options: spending less and earning more.

Now, spending less doesn't sound fun, and sometimes it isn't. But...sometimes it is! It's all about your attitude. If you treat spending less as a game or a challenge, you might be surprised at how much satisfaction you can get from getting a good deal— and you might grow to love how smart and savvy you feel.

Or you might not. In which case, you can always earn more money. You can also approach the problem from both ends, spending less and earning more. Whatever works for you is fine by me!

Tips and tricks to slenderize your spending

How do you slenderize your spending without sitting in the dark alone on Saturday night? Here are some tips and tricks to help you cut back on some of the expenses in your budget.

Commuting and travel

- Does your work reimburse you for commute or travel expenses? At my work, I have to submit a ton of paperwork to get reimbursed for public transportation costs when I go to meetings— these are meetings outside of my normal commute to and from work. It is super annoying to track $2 each time I go anywhere, but I do it quarterly and the first time I did it I was shocked that in three months I had spent $100. That's $400 a year, well worth the hour's worth of paperwork I have to do every three months. That is like making $100 an hour...more than I make at my day job, that's for sure!

- Can you carpool? This will immediately cut your costs.
- Public transportation is not the same everywhere, but do a quick google to see if there are bus or train routes that go to places you frequent. I personally would prefer a longer commute and the ability to read on the train or bus over sitting in traffic and feeling frustrated. You can also compare the actual cost of driving your car per mile— the government rate is around $.54 a mile[*], so if bus fare comes out to be cheaper, think about a bus instead.
- Can you telecommute? This cuts your commuting costs by 100%! If your boss isn't into it but it's technically allowed, pitch a one-day-per-week work at home day with a scheduled performance review. If it's going well, you'll save 20% of your commuting costs and you won't have to get dressed for work.
- Once you own a bike, riding it is free. Plus, you won't need a gym membership.
- Do you even need a car? When I moved to a big city, I sold my car and cobbled together a bunch of travel choices, depending on my energy level/the weather/how much time I had. Sometimes I walked. Sometimes I rented a bike (I lived on top of a giant hill with a lot of traffic and was too scared and would have died trying to ride up it so I only

---

[*] This calculation includes both gas and wear and tear, which is easy to forget.

ever rode downhill). Sometimes I took a bus or the subway. Sometimes I got a rideshare. Sometimes I hailed a cab. All of these transportation options were significantly cheaper than when I owned my car (don't forget the costs of gas, maintenance and car insurance) and I didn't have to deal with city parking.

- If gas prices are killing you, look into an electric car. Electric cars cost about $.04 per mile in energy. Gas cars cost about 2-5x that amount. Electric cars aren't right for everyone, but they might fit your lifestyle more than you'd think.

- Speaking of, one of the most overlooked options is the rental economy. One reason why people don't choose electric cars is because they think they might want to go on long road trips. While infrastructure is changing so long road trips in an electric car is now a real possibility, the other reality is most people go on just a few road trips per year and saving a significant amount per mile for a whole year's worth of driving will more than pay for a couple of days of rental cars. The same goes for trucks— sure, they are nice to have in case you need to move a sofa or haul things, but how much are you paying for a truck versus how often do you actually use it? Consider the rental economy as a reasonable option.

Dining out and having a social life

- Do you eat out a lot? Consider cooking at home more. Every person in the entire world finds cooking skills to be an attractive quality. Short on equipment? Goodwill has a ton of cooking equipment that costs about 10% of what you would pay for it new. Grossed out by Goodwill? How is buying a dish at Goodwill and then washing it at home any different than eating off a dish in a restaurant? Also, you are reusing an item that might otherwise end up in a landfill. Short on time? Look for a crockpot at Goodwill. Bam! Dinner is served! If you are opposed to cooking in general or seem to set the fire alarm off every time you try, buying frozen prepared foods is still cheaper than buying takeout. With God as my witness, you'll never go hungry again!

- Speaking of eating out a lot...do you pack your lunch? Make your own coffee? Why don't you whip out your new crockpot and make a week's worth of lunches at once with minimal effort? Doing things yourself can save a significant amount of money in the long run. Spending $7 on eating out at lunch every day is $1,820 a year. Spent on sub-par takeout sandwiches.
- A few people in my office started a lunch swap program. A group of five friends each made one meal with five servings each and then they swapped for a week's worth of lunches with minimal effort. Depending on what you make, this should save on groceries because you can buy in bulk and you need fewer ingredients than making five separate meals. Moms' clubs are famous for doing similar freezer meal swaps, too, which are good for everyone, not just moms!
- I love a nice grande-soy-vanilla-latte as much as the next girl. I enrolled in the rewards program for my neighborhood coffee chain, I watch the emails and sign up for deals, and about every 5th coffee is free. I don't go often— it's not a daily habit, but a coffee treat is relatively inexpensive and I love cashing in my freebies.
- Look at the menu before you agree on the restaurant. If you can't afford it, suggest an alternative.
- Sign up for Open Table and then make reservations for the group. You can earn dining points which add up to a free dining check when you have enough points.

- Pay attention to food costs— soups, salads, appetizers, sandwiches, hamburgers and pizzas are usually cheaper and can be as filling as an entrée. I can't even remember the last time I could finish a whole restaurant hamburger, so there is lunch for tomorrow, too!
- Don't drink to excess— learn to nurse your drinks. Alternating alcoholic drinks with nonalcoholic drinks will cut your bill almost in half, and you will feel better the next day.
- Cocktails are usually more expensive than wine, wine is usually pricier than beer, and craft/imported beer is usually more expensive than domestic beer. Think about how much you plan to drink, and order accordingly. Don't buy rounds for a large group unless you can afford it. If your friends are buying rounds and you can't reciprocate, don't partake. Graciously explain you are nursing what you've got, and leave if you think you'll end up charging more than you can afford.
- Look for happy hour/appetizer specials.
- Try to get separate checks when in a large group— no one intends to short the bill, but even though you would like to believe your friends all know how to add.... evidence has shown time and time again they can't. Avoid the stress when possible.
- Avoid the extras— skipping an appetizer, dessert and a drink can cut your bill in half.
- Eat before you meet your friends and then order something small or just a drink.
- Don't scrimp on tips. Serving is hard work, and your server probably can't afford his or her social life either— don't short someone else who is working hard. If you can't afford a decent tip, then you can't afford to eat out.

Looking sharp

- Buy things in the off season. Christmas wrapping paper is cheap on December 26, not so cheap on December 24. Sweaters, coats, boots— cheaper in the spring! Bathing suits, shorts, sandals— buy 'em in the fall! I have a few stores I buy the majority of my work clothes from. In exchange for getting an annoying number of emails from them, I am alerted to their quarterly sales where all clearance items are 75% off— but I'm buying winter things in spring. I only buy my clothes during these sales, and I just order a ton of things online and then return what doesn't work.
- A few months after I started working in an office, my friend organized a clothing swap. A bunch of young women cleaned out their closets (added bonus!), all got together, poured some wine and swapped clothes. This was not only super fun, but professional clothes can be very expensive and this was a good way to get new clothes without having to spend a lot of money. We donated the remaining clothes to Dress for Success.
- You can't beat the prices at Goodwill, but you also need a lot of time and patience to look good. Try an in-person or online consignment shop like ThredUP to help limit the options to quality items you are interested in.
- If you have a specific product you like (a certain brand of jeans), look for them online instead of buying them full price in stores.

Entertainment

- Evaluate your entertainment habits. Buy a lot of movies? Try checking out the selection at your library. My library has a ton of movies and tv shows on DVD, and I can download free audiobooks and eBooks and if I want the newest bestseller I can put myself on the waitlist. Do you watch your cable enough for it to be worth it, or should you buy a Netflix subscription instead? Do you have Netflix and Hulu and Amazon Prime and cable? How do you have time?! Prioritize your favorite media sources and ditch the rest— or, spend three months bingeing on each streaming service before moving on (this may be some of the best advice in the whole book, because it costs less and instead of waiting for your shows to come out you can just happily binge your favorites all year round. You're welcome.)

- Are you a book buyer? Me too. But I'm more of a book borrower, because libraries are free and wonderful community services and really should be supported.
- There is usually great local music available with no cover when you go mid-week.
- Sometimes clubs/bars will have midweek theme nights (i.e., Tuesday Funk Night, Thursday Line Dancing) you don't have to pay a cover for. They can be more fun than weekends!
- If you have clever friends, check out trivia nights. Trivia is fun, and the prize for winning is often money off your bill. Less popular trivia nights= more chances of winning for you!

Utility bills

- Turn off the lights, for Pete's sake! Actually, turning off any unused electronics, especially older TVs (a nice surge protector will make this easy with just one switch) should help lower your electric bills. Unplug anything you aren't using regularly because some electronics will suck energy even when they aren't turned on.

- Take shorter showers, turn off the faucet when you brush. Taking a four minute shower could save you up to $100 a year. Skip shampooing every day and you'll spend less on water and shampoo, and your hair will be more beautiful than ever!
- I am terrible at handwashing clothes, so I will never recommend you forgo washing machine use to save money. I will, however, recommend forgoing dryer use. At one of my apartments it cost $2 for one hour in the dryer, and my clothes were usually still damp! $4 to dry each load? Where the heck was I supposed to get all those quarters?! I bought a sturdy, large, adjustable drying rack and I expect it will last forever. At that apartment, it paid for itself in 10 loads of laundry. If you have a dryer in your home, using a drying rack will save you about $.75 per load. This doesn't sound like much, but after a year of drying one load per week your fancy clothes rack will have paid for itself. Added perk— air drying makes your clothes last longer and it is better for the environment. If you don't want to fuss about hanging clothes, at least hang your sheets over the (clean) tops of doors. Sheets are a pain to dry in the dryer anyway, and this way they dry for free!

Housing

- Sometimes moving home is a good idea. Sometimes it isn't. Treat your parents fairly and at least offer to pay rent and utilities. You aren't 14 anymore so clean your room, do chores, cook dinner and be an adult.
- The fastest way to save on housing expenses is to get a roommate. Make sure you're not breaking the terms of your lease.
- Sometimes landlords pay for things like yard maintenance. Offer to do the yardwork yourself and see if they will knock

the cost of yard work off your rent. Don't forget you need yard tools for this— but some areas (especially areas with high risk of wildfires) have free loans of mowers and weedwhackers through the local public works or fire departments.

- Before you move in, see if your landlord will do some upgrades— can you get the place painted or the appliances replaced? It never hurts to ask.
- If you know you're moving, see if your landlord will give you a bonus if you find (good) new tenants to fill your spot.
- If you're near the end of your lease, you might consider downgrading— either to a smaller place or a new neighborhood. Moving doesn't have to be expensive and whatever you're saving on rent will be 12x the savings over the course of the year.
- If you're moving to a place you think you want to stay in for a while, consider a longer term lease with a fixed rent rate. That way you can avoid any rent hikes.

Impressing your guests

- Try going potluck (one of my best themes was a "dip-off" party where everyone brought their favorite dip).
- I was recently invited to a cereal and board game party. It was so good— basically the party of my dreams. Everyone brought a box of cereal and the hostess provided milk and we all got to eat the sugar cereals from our childhoods we don't eat anymore but wish we did.
- Learning to make fancy cocktails at home is much more affordable than ordering them at bars. A girlfriend of mine hosts monthly "cocktail Fridays" and tries a new cocktail recipe every month.
- Soups, tacos, vegetarian dishes and egg-based brunch dishes are inexpensive ways to feed crowds.

- Host a movie night with frozen pizzas, beer and popcorn to save on theater costs.
- Game nights are a great way to spend time with your friends without spending a lot of cash. I especially like winter game nights because I never feel like getting dressed up for cold weather and navigating bars with a coat.
- If your house isn't available for hosting, consider hosting picnics in public parks (check local laws before bringing alcohol).
- Having a party? Embarrassed about not buying nicer wine and/or your sad liquor selection? Try making a crowd-pleasing sangria with some box wine (yum yum yum yum). Or, for wintertime dranks— mulled wine! Ask guests to BYOB for dinners or house parties to keep your alcohol costs low.
- Go for some crowd-pleasing cheap eats, but put some thought into them. I have a killer six-bean veggie chili recipe I serve with a baked potato bar— including bacon, cheddar, sour cream, scallions, caramelized onions etc. etc. The topping options (which can top either the potatoes or the chili) makes the whole meal seem a little fancier, and feeding a crowd on beans and potatoes won't break the bank, leaves vegetarians happy, and fills up my guests.

General shopping tips

- Buy things when they are on sale. My favorite razors are on sale this week for half the cost of what they usually are. I bought multiple packages, because I know I will use them eventually and I would rather not run out and then have to pay a higher price.
- Stop buying bottled water. It costs $.08 per year to drink tap water for all your water needs. Eight cents. You can find that lying on the street. Fussy about water? Buy

yourself a Brita, sign up for Amazon to automatically order you filter refills on a schedule, get yourself a few reusable water bottles and stop wasting money and plastic.

- When you buy online, check out retailmenot.com for online coupon codes all compiled in one place. Pretty handy.
- Buy bulk. Not a good option if you live in NYC, but if you have the storage space it is better to pay $.40 per roll of toilet paper in that ginormous pack than it is to pay $.80 per roll for the tiny pack. Plus, you run out less frequently and that is always good (and you save on gas because you have fewer trips to the store). I hate buying toilet paper. It just feels like I am flushing my money away! (yuk yuk yuk). Keep in mind: don't assume bulk stores are always cheaper because sometimes sales at normal stores lower the price further than a standard price at a bulk store.
- Check out the perks that go along with things you already have. I get 10% off train tickets (something I use quite a bit) and discounted movie tickets with my AAA membership. I get a certain percent off purchases I make with my credit card when I go through the credit card's website to get to the store's website rather than just going directly to the store's website.
- Can you extend the amount of time between recurring expenses? I love getting pedicures, but instead of getting them every month like I would like to, I get them every 6 weeks instead. After 3 weeks I do a quick refresher coat on my own, which doesn't look as good but it definitely doesn't look as bad as chipped polish. Now you know intimate details about my toes. You're welcome.

This list is called "Tips and Tricks" not "Do This Because Kate Said To." If you don't have space to dry your clothes— don't worry about it! You can cut back in another area. You love Netflix and Hulu and Amazon Prime? That's ok! Try making your own lunches for work instead of cancelling your

Netflix subscription. The point is— make your budget work for you. Cutting back on expenses isn't fun, but managing your expenses is a judgment call and you are the boss of your own finances, so only you can decide what to cut and what to leave.

Eating on a budget: the no ramen plan

I really like to eat.

I watch the Great British Baking Show (and not just for Paul Hollywood, that silver fox). I buy cookbooks for the photos, I subscribe to cooking magazines, my Zagat guide is full of notes from new restaurants I have tried.

I like cooking, I like being cooked for, I like eating out, I like hearing about recipes and I really like taste testing.

This habit can become expensive.

I try not to eat ramen...but there have been times in my life when I could hardly even afford that. What was a poor kid with a developed palate to do?

I had to learn to cook at home— and not only to learn to cook at home, but to learn to cook meals that a. I love and b. don't break my supermarket budget (and optional c. impress my dinner guests. Having dinner at home saves on restaurant bills!) Knowing how to cook is a trait everyone finds sexy— cooking at home will not only decrease the cost of food, but it will up your sex appeal. (Is the oven making it hot in here or is that just you? Oh baby.)

Here are some general tips that will help you slenderize your grocery budget:

Coupons. Oh coupons. Paper coupons have always been kind of a hassle to keep track of, and unless you're an extreme couponer I'm not sure they are worth the effort. If you have time and energy and interest, there are extreme coupon groups in most places in the US— give it a whirl if you want to! Just don't fall for the trap of buying things because they are cheap. Buying something you don't want or won't eat for 75% off is still wasting your money. Also, don't forget your time has value. If you're spending ten hours a week to clip coupons and go to multiple stores to save $50…maybe you could have figured out a different way to earn $50 in ten hours instead.

Coupon alternatives. What I do recommend instead of paper couponing is you sign up for your grocery store's discount card program online and then see if there are extra promotions available online beyond the regular ones you get with just owning a card. I have access to internet coupons that load directly onto my grocery card, and it takes me about five minutes to prep for my shopping trip. My grocery card not only gives me coupons on things you can't get from normal newspaper coupons (discounts on produce, fresh bakery items, meat), but they also track my purchases so I get special deals on the items I buy the most. I can upload my list of coupons to my phone so I can double check that I have the brand right while I am in the store. For five minutes of work, I save 20-30% each time I go grocery shopping. It's slightly annoying to get it set up (but really only takes 10 minutes) and I have saved hundreds of dollars on groceries this year.

Meal planning. I was so resistant to meal planning because I like to think of myself as a spontaneous and creative cook, but what I was really doing was creating a ton of work, waste, and maintaining a ridiculously overstuffed pantry for no good reason. Meal planning has saved my family a ton of money, made grocery shopping easier, and I no longer have to duck when I open my pantry door. I make it a point to try a brand new recipe every week, which has kept things interesting. I also only plan meals I like and it's nice to have a meal I'm looking forward to eating *every single night.*

Grocery pickup. This goes super well with meal planning. My local grocery store has an app that allows me to shop online, and then I schedule a time to pick up. It's free, it's super easy, I don't impulse buy and I never forget items. It's also super handy when you run out of milk to just order it as soon as you run out rather than having to remember what is in your fridge in the middle of the grocery store.

Bulk buying. Think carefully when buying in bulk. Do you cook for one? What are you going to do with 10 lbs. of bananas that were on super sale at Costco? Buying bulk for things that don't spoil quickly (onions, potatoes, squash, peanut butter) = good. Making 12 loaves of banana bread because you couldn't eat those bananas in time = defeats the purpose of saving by buying bulk. But wait! Do you have a friend or roommate who is also on a food budget? Buying in bulk and then splitting the haul is an excellent solution— especially if only one of you has a bulk store membership.

Seconds stores. Some grocery stores have massively cheap, fresh and amazing produce. These stores carry "seconds," which are fruits and veggies that have been rejected by the major groceries but are still fresh and good to eat. If a box of apples has one rotten apple, it is likely the whole box will end up at the seconds store for a fraction of the price. Awesome deal, but I don't have any hard and fast rule about where to find the stores that carry seconds— usually they are local ethnic stores or those weird off-brand groceries where sometimes you have to pay a quarter to get a cart. I guess you just have to be adventurous in your grocery explorations!

More tips

- Shop the sales. If broccoli is on sale this week and cauliflower is not...this might be a broccoli week, my friend.
- Buy meat in bulk and freeze it in usable portions.
- Generally, not wasting food will save you money. Cooking at home without being wasteful is a challenge. Sometimes I am better at this than other times. Making an effort to rotate my fridge, freezing leftovers I can't stand to look at anymore, and doing some meal planning can all help reduce your waste (and can give me some ready-to-eat lunches for later on, which is another money saving tip!)
- If you don't already, buy generic. Usually generic brands are made by the same manufacturer as name brand so you are getting the exact same product. I haven't found much difference between the two.

Food choices

- Beans are given a bad rap. Sometimes they stink (hehe literally...get it?). But sometimes beans are creamy, or garlicky, or spicy, or smoky. Beans are high in fiber and are an excellent source of protein.
- Eggs! What a fantastic, versatile, filling, cheap food. You can eat eggs at every meal. They are so comforting and delicious. They can be a convenience food (hard boiled) or a gourmet food (poached in white wine, fancy!), food for a crowd (quiche) or comfort food (scrambled with buttered toast). Excellent invention, chickens! A dozen eggs costs less than a latte and it can feed you a number of meals for a week.
- Think about buying and using meat as a seasoning rather than as the main entree. Meat is usually the most expensive item people buy, but you can use it for flavor and get your protein elsewhere to stretch your budget without going totally veggie. For example— I make this absolutely

delicious meal with butternut squash, white beans, kale, polenta and bacon. The whole dish uses three strips of bacon and the flavor is fantastic. Bacon, sausage and ham all have a strong flavor punch, especially in soup.

- Bargain produce to consider eating more of: bananas, cabbage (seriously! great on tacos, in stir fry, cole slaw, stuffed cabbage, cabbage soup), potatoes, sweet potatoes, squash and carrots. Frozen produce also can be a bargain. Don't forget to buy seasonal produce to get the best deals and the best quality produce!
- Try growing your own herbs. Dried herbs are expensive (and not as tasty), but fresh herbs will cost you your entire paycheck. Each herb plant should be $3-$4 at a garden store and will keep producing (just don't kill it, obviously). Thrifty superstar tip? Save any mint you get as a garnish. Take it home and put it in water. Plant it when it grows roots. There you go! Free mint forever. (Plant in a pot, don't plant it in your yard, it is invasive and you will never be rid of it.)
- I would recommend growing your own vegetables, but as a hobbyist veggie gardener myself I know this hobby sometimes costs more than I get out of it in produce so don't start a veggie garden expecting to save money on your first try. Go for it if you think it'll be a fun hobby, because it is!
- Make your own chicken, turkey or veggie stock. This is easy to do— after you roast a chicken (significantly easier than you think it will be, I promise!), save the bones and boil them for a few hours with some salt and vegetables like onion, carrots and celery. My best no-waste trick is to save the little bits of veggies you won't eat when you're cooking for other meals (like the ends of carrots or onions, or celery leaves), put them in the freezer, and when you are ready to

make stock use those instead of putting in whole good vegetables.

- You can avoid buying green onions if you save the white ends and let them sprout in water.
- Hard and semi soft cheese is the only food you can safely just slice the mold right off and keep eating. (Is that gross? My dad told me that trick and I haven't gotten sick yet. Blue cheese is half mold anyway so it must be ok.)
- Freeze fruit that has a weird texture or produce that is almost spoiled that you won't eat in time. Make some smoothies, put the veggies into soup, bake the fruit into oatmeal or rice pudding, or make a pie. I just made an amazing pot of applesauce with a few disgustingly mealy apples.
- Depending on your milk consumption, consider buying more expensive organic milk— it tends to have an expiration date a few weeks after non-organic milk (my dairy industry friend says it has to do with freshness and shipping). When I buy normal milk I usually have to toss half of it, when I buy organic I am more likely to finish it before it expires. It costs more up front but it saves me money over time, plus I waste less.
- Chicken with bones in and skin on is cheaper than boneless skinless. It takes about 5 minutes of grossness to peel the skin off chicken and it saves a lot of money. I personally think bone in chicken is always tastier because it makes the meat more tender (and you can save the bones to make stock, you clever bean!)
- Soup is (with the exception of lobster bisque) a bargain meal that is lovely in the wintertime.
- Lots of inexpensive foods (beans, eggs, cabbage, sweet potato) tastes better as a taco. You know what else is inexpensive? Tortillas. Yum.

Make mo' cash money

You're tracking your spending, you've set up your budget, you're slenderizing your spending...but still, things aren't adding up. The alternative to spending less is to make more, but sometimes your lifestyle just isn't conducive to switching jobs or adding another job into the mix of awesomeness that is your life.

There are a few ways to increase your income that don't require major lifestyle changes. It all depends what you are looking for, so choose what works for you.

Some ideas:

- Are you a cat whisperer, dog whisperer or baby whisperer? Try pet sitting or babysitting. Worked to bring in money when you were 14, still works to bring in money now.
- I used to work as a caterer for super fancy weddings when I was in college. They were almost all on Saturday nights in the spring and summer, so it didn't interfere with my weekday schoolwork and activities. I was in a pool of servers so if I couldn't work then they would just call the next person on the list. Unlike normal serving, you make pretty high base pay, everyone is eating the same thing so it's really easy and you also get tips. The whole event takes between 8-10 hours. Not too bad. Just don't spill lobster on the mother of the bride like I did my first day.
- Are you a math whiz? A master wordsmith? In love with history? Somewhere out there, there is a student struggling in the subject you loved and he or she has parents who are willing to pay to help that kid get an A. Get into tutoring! You can sign up with a local tutoring company, post on Craigslist or on local college websites (or email professors) or drop flyers off at local school. The pay is awesome, the hours are flexible, and you are helping someone out.

- Do you have a hobby? Could that hobby turn into money? Crafty or artsy people might want to open up an Etsy shop or contract out a booth at a local fair or festival. Musical people (depending on the instrument and your level of skill) might want to play for weddings or funerals. Be creative— I love refinishing furniture I find at yard sales. I've sold some of my furniture for profit after I had rescued it and refinished it. I didn't have to set up a store, I just sold it on Craigslist and enjoyed doing the work!
- Many churches need help only on Sunday mornings. Sometimes they need help with childcare or they need someone to come in early to turn on lights and heat and make coffee. This is another job that won't interfere with your weekday schedule! Check out your local churches and other religious institutions in the area.
- What do you do at your day job? Could you sell those services as an independent consultant? (make sure you aren't breaking any rules at your work, please). I got paid to format my friend's PhD dissertation because I am a whiz at word documents, thanks to my nitpicky admin experience. Once I had done one dissertation I had the tricky formatting rules down and I could have marketed myself as the PhD dissertation formatting expert of the university (but I had other life plans for myself so I didn't!).
- Are you a computer master? Can you make websites? People pay a lot of cash money for those skills.
- Look around your house. Do you have a lot of stuff? Books, board games, nice clothes, electronics, DVDs, sports equipment...pretty much anything you are tired of that is in good shape can be sold. Try selling it on Craigslist, Facebook marketplace, OfferUp or set up an eBay account— just keep in mind eBay charges fees and shipping expenses can add up, so if the item is listed for too low of a price it might not be worth your time.

- Neat freak? Offer your cleaning or organizational services for a fee.
- If you have a flexible schedule but just aren't ready to commit to a permanent job, try temping. There are always a ton of administrative jobs that anyone with basic computer skills, attention to detail and customer service skills can do. Sometimes the jobs are temp-to-hire so if you are a good fit for the company and if you like the job they might hire you on full time. Otherwise, it can help keep the lights on while you are waiting for your dream job to come through or for school to start up again. A benefit is you get to work in a variety of offices and see what different workplaces are like. You also can pick up some skills that look great on a resume.
- Own a truck? Try offering your services as a moving assistant.
- I had a friend who started her own company as a "helper." If you need help prepping for a party— she will help you! If you need help going grocery shopping— call her up! Need someone to help you wash dishes because you have a new baby and who knew breast pumps have a million parts that need hand washing twelve times a day? She is the woman for you! It is a lovely idea for a side business.

The main point of these ideas is that there are ways to supplement your income if you are willing to work for them. Play to your strengths— I hate babysitting so I will never advertise my babysitting services. I love working with people so I don't mind answering phones for the day as a temp. Be creative about how you get the word out about your new endeavors— Craigslist, bulletin boards, word of mouth— they all work well.

If you are job hunting, here is my last piece of advice. Get out there and volunteer in the field you are trying to get into. It will get you out of the house, it will give you experience and references you can put on a resume, and it will help other people. It may or may not lead to a permanent job (don't go into volunteering expecting to get a job in return)— but meeting more people, letting them know you are looking for a job and getting experience is always a good plan. For a while I volunteered a few hours every Friday at a museum where I created educational material for the public. Guess what real job I got hired for a few months later? A job making educational materials for the public (not at the same place I volunteered at, but this time I got a lovely salary!) I got the job because I already had experience! You never know where volunteering will lead you.

If there isn't a formal volunteer program in the field you want to work in, try to create your own position. People generally say yes to enthusiastic and motivated free help. Even a few hours a week counts as experience.

You won't get rich off these ideas (well, maybe you will, in which case you are cleverer than I!) but hopefully they will take some of the pressure off your finances while you are out living your awesome life.

A word about Multi-Level Marketing (MLM)

You know what this is— your friends trying to sell you essential oils or miracle hair care. I am temporarily in a spot where many women are severely underemployed, so MLM is rampant. There are some good things about MLM— it can supplement your income, give you satisfaction, help you to socialize. There are also some bad things about MLM— you're using your friendships for profit, you're part of a pyramid scheme, you sometimes have to purchase product upfront and many of the marketing techniques are based on fearmongering.

I'm not going to pass judgement on MLM, but if you are thinking about MLM here are a few things to consider: women make up the majority of people who participate in

MLM. Women are traditionally underpaid and underemployed, and while MLM does provide flexibility there is also a huge amount of time and risk involved. MLM employees do all the marketing and legwork. It's hard to get a clear answer about the amount of time and energy it takes to succeed at MLM, but most successful salespeople manage a "team" of salespeople underneath them, who are also encouraged to manage their own "teams." (This is a classic pyramid scheme and the enthusiasm of your friends about their success stems directly from the fact that they make more if you sign on, too). When I see companies set up pyramid schemes that target traditionally underemployed and underpaid populations, I like to think about *why* they have chosen this business plan and who will be profiting.

MLM might be a good choice for you and your family, but it also might not be. If you know your market value and you have done your research and think that MLM will be a path that will compensate you fairly, go for it. But be aware that MLM business plans can also be exploitative and tough on friendships. Make sure you are earning appropriate compensation for your work.

Takeaway actions and ideas:

This chapter is full of tips for cutting your spending and ways to earn a little cash on the side. You have to read it to get the goods.

Chapter 9: Life hacks

Handling the holidays

Mulled cider, cozy fires, wrapping presents, cookies...holidays are great. Unless they break the bank and cause massive amounts of stress. Holiday finances can be tough because you're often expected to travel at peak times, there may not be space for you to stay with family, you have to buy presents...and it comes once a year, so it is incredibly difficult to budget for.

Not to mention the tricky navigation of balancing divorced parents and in-laws and the gross guilt/relief when you just don't want to see some of your family. How can you make the holidays as pain free as possible? Here are some tips.

Gift giving

Gifts are a fun part of the holiday season, but they are also high stress and highly expensive and there will come a time in your life you just don't need anything else. At some point, you should have a candid talk with your family about reducing the stress from gift giving— and there are a number of ways to maintain the fun and surprise of the season without having to go all out. Here are some suggestions:

- Secret Santa with a budget cap— you only have to buy one gift and you know the amount you will be expected to spend. Pro tip: if you suggest and run a Secret Santa, you also can be the first to suggest a budget so you're more likely to get your way.
- Food presents— no one needs more stuff, everyone loves food. Make homemade bread, cookies, spiced nuts, homemade jerky... whatever floats your boat. Not much of a baker? Look up dried soup mixes, dip pretzels in chocolate or make homemade seasoned popcorn. A nice six-pack or a

bottle of wine you personally have enjoyed is a good gift too. It doesn't have to be fancy to be yummy.

- No-new-things holidays. This works great for a gift swap game too. Everyone involved agrees to either give away something they already own, regift (carefully! Remember who it is from originally!) or buy something from a thrift store.
- Books. Nearly all books are affordable, and there is a book out there that will interest everyone on your list. Bonus: books are exceptionally easy to wrap, unlike that new bocce set. Don't you think someone in your family needs a copy of a personal finance book?
- Activities or services. Instead of physical gifts, try giving out experiences like researching historic areas of your city and then giving tours, or spend the day looking for the best donut in your town. Family members will also appreciate the gift of closet organization, free auntie/uncle babysitting, or offering to detail a car.
- There was an episode of Seinfeld where George gives all his friends the gift of a donation to "The Human Fund," which was not a real charity. Of course he gets found out because he's George Costanza, but you can actually make charitable donations in honor of loved ones and give the donation as a gift. Alternatively, you can pledge to volunteer a certain number of hours in honor of the gift recipient. Don't forget to follow through!

Travel

- Could your family do a holiday re-enactment on a less busy travel weekend, like Veterans Day? This will keep you from traveling during peak times and should lower everyone's stress levels.

- If you have different family branches you feel obligated to see, try to set up an agreement with your family/in laws so you alternate years. As your generation ages and get married, it's going to be harder and harder to coordinate with cousins and siblings. If you can get everyone on the same alternating years schedule, you can make sure to see everyone all together and avoid holiday FOMO.
- Accept offers from people around you. The first time I had to miss a family Thanksgiving I was devastated. I love Thanksgiving and I just couldn't imagine having a nice day without my family around me. A friend invited me to her family's home for their meal and I ended up having the best time. Her mom had bought huge tupperwares specifically for the "orphan" guests so we could all have leftovers and I remember how kind they were and how welcome I felt. I missed my family, but not even close to as much as I expected. Remember to be a good guest and bring a dish and/or a host/hostess gift when you're welcomed into a family holiday.

Too-many-houseguests syndrome

Too many houseguests, not enough beds? As you get older, sleeping on the couch in a crowded house loses its appeal, but hotels can be expensive. If you feel like there's no room at the inn, check for local Airbnbs or reach out to friends who live in the area who might be traveling themselves to see if they would be cool with you staying at their place for a few days. Worst case scenario, make your trip a little shorter than it might have been otherwise.

Budgeting for the holidays

The other hard part about the holidays is budgeting for them. Even if you give thoughtful, inexpensive gifts, you're still pretty much guaranteed to have guessed wrong about the costs. Here are a few tricks I recommend for socking away a little extra cash for the season:

- Open up a 12-month certificate of deposit (CD) in December. Your bank will have these so just look around the website. CDs are accounts where you put your money to earn higher interest than a savings account, but you can't get the money out early without paying a penalty. Set an automatic amount to contribute each month. When it matures next December, you'll have a nice little budget that has been earning interest all year!
- If you aren't in credit card debt, save your rewards points from all your expenses for the year until the holiday season. Your rewards are really a bonus, so spending them should not impact your regular budget or even your bank account. Pro tip: many credit cards will let you stretch your rewards even further if you shop through the rewards website.
- A separate bank account. If you don't mind managing multiple accounts, set up a holiday fund account and automatically move money every month. Try to earn a high interest rate. This is similar to a CD except you will have penalty-free access to your money at any point during the year if you have an emergency come up and you'll probably earn lower interest than with a CD. Try not to tap into this account or else you might have a sad chicken breast for Thanksgiving dinner instead of a glorious turkey.

Remember holidays and holiday traditions are only good if they aren't causing you stress and worry the other eleven months of the year. Think about what you want from your holidays, and focus on the love and sharing around the holiday season instead of on gifts and spending.

Moving on the cheap

In my twenties, I moved over nineteen times.

I believe that makes me a moving expert.

Some people think moving is very expensive. It can be! But it doesn't have to be, and lucky you, you have the world's foremost leading moving expert writing to you about how to move without spending all your money.

Here are some tricks:

- Do not ever, ever, ever pay for moving boxes. You are killing trees and you are wasting money. Instead (start this a few weeks early)— go to the grocery stores in your area, preferably early in the morning. Ask them for apple boxes (they are the best because they are super sturdy and they have lids). Bat your eyelashes. Keep asking. Ask when their shipments come in. Collect the boxes. Alternatively, if you have access to paper boxes that are used in an office or a copy center— get those! Those are even better! Also, sometimes people post about moving boxes on the free section of Craigslist— that is a good source for many boxes at once. It takes a little running around, but it is worth it.
- This is my mom's advice: Go to the gym. Make friends with people who like picking up heavy things for fun. My mother is a genius.
- This is my advice: Try to maintain a friendship with someone who owns a truck. Bake them cookies in exchange for an afternoon with their truck. Don't forget to fill the tank.
- Help a friend move and have them promise to help you move. Well worth it.

- Don't leave behind the stupid things you think you don't want to pack, like your trash cans or your clothes hangers or your shower curtain. I promise wherever you are moving to will not have those things and you will have to go buy more. Worse than moving a trash can is spending money on a new one when you just had a perfectly good one of your own.
- Clean out your closets before you move, especially if you are shipping things. Yard sales or selling online can be an added source of cash that can help you get rid of the unwanted items clogging up your house.
- Speaking of shipping— if you live near an Amtrak station and are moving near another Amtrak station, Amtrak is the best shipping deal in the entire world. The prices are variable so you have to check their website for pricing, but when I moved across the country I shipped 17 boxes for $350 total and it took four days to travel across the country. They won't ship a number of items (like furniture or electronics) but they are a great deal if your stuff qualifies. You have to pick the boxes up in person at the end station rather than get them delivered to your house, but at that price, you can afford a rental truck.
- If you are shipping a bike, go to your local bike store and ask them for any spare bike boxes they might have. New ones are about $20, spare ones are free. Watch a video on how to pack a bike for shipping— bike shops will charge anywhere from $75 to $200 to pack a bike for you, but you can do the whole process for free in about a half hour (make sure you have the right tools on hand). I have not yet figured out how to safely put bikes back together on my own, but that is what bike shops and/or savvy friends who will help with your bike in exchange for beer are for.
- Trying to buy used furniture? Craigslist and Facebook Marketplace are good but require a lot of coordination.

Yard sales (early in the morning=better haul) can be awesome for getting a whole lot of stuff in one day (and one time I got a free bottle of wine at a yard sale. Long story. Horrible wine.) Goodwill and other used furniture places can be good too, but they can be variable depending on where you live. I also have had amazing luck with online estate sale auctions, although the websites are often sketchalicious— for my last move I bought two dressers, a shelf, two nightstands and a mirror for less than $90. I also had great luck with the Habitat for Humanity ReStore, which is essentially a discount home improvement store that also carries used furniture. They take donations and all proceeds go to Habitat for Humanity. I just bought a beautiful hardwood hutch and hardwood shelf for $85 total. And I supported one of my favorite charities. Nice.

- It is easier to clean a place before you move all your things in. Just saying.
- When you move out, ask your landlords if they are going to have a cleaning service come in or if you can do it instead. Sometimes landlords will pay for a professional cleaning service out of your safety deposit (this will be in your lease)— see if you can do it yourself and make sure you get a walkthrough with the landlord so you both agree your cleaning was up to snuff. If they are going to get professionals in anyway, don't bother the cozy dust bunnies.
- When you move in, take pictures of any damage on the house already and then email it to your landlord so you are both on the same page. When you are moving in it seems so obvious the damage is already there (or it might not even appear to be damage), but when you move out the landlord may try to charge you for it. Once my landlord tried to charge me $200 because the residents before me had nailed a shelf to the wall. I didn't think it was considered

"damage" because it was there when I got there— but apparently the landlord forgot who the culprit was. Save yourself the annoyance and take pictures of the rooms when you get there.

- Think about long-term vs. temporary when you are decorating a rental. New art for the walls you take with you when you go= good. New chandelier for the rental house because you think the old one is ugly= bad investment. Remember this is temporary and you can live with an ugly chandelier for a while.
- If you know you are moving, plan early. Start looking for boxes a few weeks ahead. Start sorting and packing with time to spare. Moving sucks but packing at 3 am the night before an all day move sucks even worse.
- Don't forget to eat. You have no food in the house and you have no plates and no silverware so it is easy to forget and then no one is happy. I have a wonderful memory of buying one of those huge self-serve frozen yogurts after moving into a house in Atlanta in August. No froyo has ever tasted as good since.
- Instead of worrying about breaking down or recycling your boxes, why don't you post on the free section of Craigslist that you have moving boxes available and pay it forward a bit?

Quick tips for tipping

It has come to my attention that many of my favorite humans on this planet do not know how to calculate a tip.

For my international readers, when you receive service at a restaurant in the US, you are expected to tip 15-20% for the service. Waitstaff make the majority of their income on tips, so it is important to make sure you are leaving enough. You can leave less if the service is horrible, but often it is not the server's fault. It is best to be generous of wallet and spirit, especially in diners where the food is cheap and the work is hard.

Don't forget that a tip can add significantly to your bill, so when you're choosing a restaurant within your price range remember to calculate in the tip.

Calculating a tip can be stressful (especially if you are trying to impress your dreamy date while trying to carry on charming conversation while also attempting to do mental math) but I can make it a little easier for you.

Quick tips for fast tip calculating:

1. Move the decimal over one spot to the left. Then approximately double. This will leave you with a tip around 20%.

For example:

   Bill is $52.67.

   Move the decimal left one spot= $5.26

   Approximately double= $10 tip. This is a 18.9% tip.

Another example:

   Bill is $78.32

   Move the decimal left one spot = $7.80, I would round to $8 just for quick mental math's sake.

   Double= $16 tip. This is a 20.4% tip.

It's not hard. They key is not to worry being exact— if you just move the decimal over and then pick an easy number to round to then double, you will be close to 20%. Under is still in the acceptable 15-20% range, and if you go over I promise your server won't complain!

2. Trick 2: use your taxes.

This only works in some states/counties. If your state taxes between 7.5-10% (it usually says it right on the bill), you can just double the amount you paid in taxes and you will be in the right range.

For example:

> Say I am in Tennessee. I pay 9.25% in sales tax. My bill comes and it looks like this:
>
> Meal: $47.15
>
> Tax (9.25%): $4.36
>
> Double the tax— you get about $8. That is a 16.9% tip— solidly in your range. Maybe add an extra buck to be generous, but you don't have to.

See? Not so bad! And your date never needs to know you didn't calculate the tip down to the last penny.

Other tipping standards that you should be paying attention to:

- Tip your bartenders $1 per drink
- Tip any sort of beauty service (nails, haircut etc.) 15-20%
- Delivery: 10%
- Anyone who carries luggage for you: $1-$5, depending on the amount of luggage
- Hotel housekeeping: $5 daily

• Valet parking: $1-$5

Also be aware that it is customary to tip generously around the holidays to anyone who provides service for you on a regular basis throughout the year.

Paying for a gym membership

I am a yoga addict. The benefits are plentiful— increased flexibility, lower stress levels, great strength training, better body awareness...I'm obsessed! (Just ask my poor husband: every time he has an ailment I tell him yoga will fix it).

Downward dog is wonderful, but paying $20 per drop in class is not. I find paying for a month up front isn't a better deal either— I just feel stressed about not going enough and wasting my money, and more stress is not what yoga is for! I do believe physical fitness is an area worth spending money on, if it makes you more likely to stick to healthy habits. I sometimes do free yoga YouTube videos at home.... but by "sometimes" I mean it's happened twice in the past year. History shows the free version is not going to work for me, so it is worth it for me to spend a little money.

Compounding the conundrum is the fact that getting to the nearest yoga studio would add an hour to my work out every time I go (car free living has a few downsides). I usually don't have a spare hour in addition to my yoga time, so the chances of me going to that studio are slim.... what to do?

There is a gym on my block that has a few yoga classes each week. The gym itself isn't especially appealing to me (rows of machines staring at blank walls, I'd rather be outside!) but the unlimited yoga for a relatively low monthly rate is just what I'm looking for.

I stopped in at the gym and asked about their rates. This gym's claim to fame is if you pay an upfront fee, you don't have to sign a contract. You pay a month-to-month rate, but you can quit at any time. This sounded pretty reasonable to me, because I do know unused gym memberships are a major way Americans waste money. I also found out there is a plan where I could pay a slightly lower monthly rate, but I would have to commit to a year. Here are the options:

- Pay $99 up front and then pay $35 a month for as long as you want to be a member. No commitments here!
- $30 a month but commit to paying $360 for the year.

Because I am me, I decided to crunch some numbers. I have already decided I miss going to yoga, and I am going to spend some money to bring yoga back into my workout routine. Drop-in classes at the not-really-near-ish yoga studio are $20 each. Do I want to keep it flexible (yuk yuk) and not commit? Or should I commit to a year?

Check out my month-by-month analysis:

Month	Cost of gym with no contract	Cost of gym with year commitment
1	$134	$30
2	$169	$60
3	$204	$90
4	$239	$120
5	$274	$150
6	$309	$180
7	$344	$210
8	$379	$240
9	$414	$270
10	$449	$300
11	$484	$330
12	$519	$360

At no point is joining the gym without a contract cheaper on a per-month basis. The first month alone costs $134! If you quit the gym any time before 7 months of membership, you will have paid less than the $360 needed for a year's membership....so you would be spending less than the $360 you've committed to, but you also would have been paying a much higher rate for those 7 months ($50 a month!).

After 7 months of membership, you are just plain overpaying. What might seem like a good deal at first (no commitments! How appealing!) is actually just a scheme to keep you from realizing paying for 7 months of "no commitments" will cost you the same as 12 months on a contract...and signing a contract is like getting 5 months of gym time free!

I decided the $360 up front is the best deal for me. $360 is the equivalent of 18 drop-in classes at the near-ish studio- so if I go to three classes every two months I will be breaking even.

Pay attention to membership options and do a little number crunching on your own. Sometimes you're paying more than you think because the marketing is intentionally tricky!

Takeaway actions and ideas:

This chapter is full of life hacks for dealing with money and the holidays, moving, tipping, and gym fees.

Chapter 10: College and graduate school tips

Getting edumacated...or not.

If you're at a point where you don't know what to do with your life, you might consider going to school to learn some things while you're figuring stuff out.

This is an ok thing to do. It can be life changing and perfect— getting a degree or two may lead you directly into a career that is a great fit and leave you with a life path to contentment.

It also sometimes is life changing the other way, if you don't have much clarity at graduation and are now saddled with a lot of student loan debt.

Do you need to go to school to meet your goals?

Here are some things to think about before you sign up for more education and the loans that (often) come along with it:

Do you know what career path you want to take? Do you know what skills you need? Is the career actually a good fit for the lifestyle you want in the future? Do you know how saturated the market is with people with your training and skills? Do you know how much money you will expect to make? (I'm about to tell you how to find these answers out so don't worry!)

The Bureau of Labor Statistics publishes one of the most useful guidebooks in America, called the Occupational Outlook Handbook— it's online so just search for it. In the OOH is an abundance of knowledge that will help you get where you want to go. Here's what you can find in there:

- A gazillion job titles
- Descriptions of the jobs
- Explanations of educational requirements
- Training or experience requirements
- Projected number of new jobs
- Median pay
- Projected growth rate in the field

I don't think I have to explain to you how helpful this information is if you are thinking about investing in a career.

Once you've researched your career path and the work you need to put in to get started, it's time to talk about money. Once you are accepted into school but before you sign anything, put together a reasonable estimate of how much the degree will cost (the financial aid office should have tuition, fees and estimated cost of living information on their website). Before you pay for a degree, do a little number crunching to figure out how long it will take you to pay back any loans you take out. Here are the things you should be looking for:

- Will your skills be in demand when you graduate? Check out the OOH.
- How good is your school's job placement history? If there is an exam requirement like passing the bar or medical certification, how well do students from your program usually do?
- Does your career field have an emphasis on networking and name recognition? (MBA programs and law schools usually fall into this category). If so, is the school you got accepted to prestigious enough to get you the contacts you want?
- What are the average starting salaries for people in your program? Check with career services if you can't find this information online.

- How much do people in your field usually make over time? Look at websites like LinkedIn and Glassdoor for realistic estimates.
- Is this job a good fit for your skills, goals and personality? I don't want to work 16 hour days. Lawyers usually have to work insane hours, at least at first. Even though I am good at research and analysis, I don't want the lifestyle that comes along with being a lawyer. Meet with people in the field for a coffee to talk about the things they like best and the things they like worst about their jobs.

See if you can lower the costs of school

You know how much school will cost, but there are strategies for lowering those expenses. Once you've been accepted but right before the acceptance deadline, call your program and tell them you are a highly competitive student. Mention any other schools you've been accepted to (name drop all you can! Don't be shy!) and if anyone has given you a scholarship mention you've been offered money at other programs. Tell them you want to go to their school, but you need to make a good financial choice.

At this particular period in time, schools have offered scholarships to students who have chosen other programs, so they should have wiggle room in their scholarship budgets to offer you funding (assuming you really are competitive. Make a case for yourself!)

Also consider feeder programs, such as a community college. Your bachelor's degree can cost significantly less if you do half your classes at a low-cost program, but make sure the credits will transfer.

Once you're in school (provided you are a good student), ask your department or advisor to help you find scholarships or career-related jobs. Be willing to try new things and speak up for your financial needs. It'll pay off in the long run.

Crunch your numbers

You've estimated how much your degree will cost and you've got an estimate for what you expect to make the first few years after earning your degree. How long will it take for you to pay back your loans? Use an online loan calculator to estimate repayment amounts. There isn't a right answer as to how much is too much, but consider how you would feel about spending that amount of money every month to deal with your student loan debts, especially considering your expected earnings once you graduate.

Finally, think about your life now and how a degree will impact your earnings. If you're at a dead-end job, this might be a good path for you to move forward in a direction you're interested in. If you're in a field that doesn't require additional education, maybe finding a mentor or getting more specific work experience is a better choice for you.

There's more to an education than money, but completely ignoring the financial aspects of getting an education could leave you in a tough position when you're just starting out.

Ok, so you've decided to go to school. Great! School is great and life changing but it can also be hard if you are scrimping pennies and your roommates have trust funds. If this is hard for you (it was for me), check out chapter 14, where I talk about reasons people have money and why it's only ever helpful to focus on your own financial situation.

Here are some tips to deal with two tricky parts of school— buying textbooks and planning spring break when you're broke.

It's textbook buying time!

Buying textbooks is stressful and risky. This is because:

- You probably aren't certain of which classes you are taking. If you buy your books too early, you might drop the class and be stuck with the book. Too late, and you are behind in your reading.
- Some professors (if you are a professor and you do this, stop it) don't really assign reading for their classes. They make you buy a book and then they don't ever once reference the reading in class and you suspect they never actually read it themselves. Some professors make you buy whole books and then only assign a chapter or two. Alternatively, some professors assign "optional" reading books that aren't actually useful at all (I'm looking at you, Greek-Mythology-Book-Assigned-to-My Contemporary-Art-History-Class). This is a massively frustrating waste of time and money.
- You will basically always lose money on your textbooks. There is no textbook website in the world that is not making a huge profit off reselling your textbooks.
- The university bookstore is the most expensive place to buy your textbooks. It is also temptingly convenient and the books look so nice and fresh and right there.
- Each textbook can cost the same amount as your grocery budget for a month. Your student years are probably the time in your life you are the poorest (hopefully things will only get better from here). This is a stinky fact of studenthood.
- Buy or rent? Download the e-book? There are a lot of decisions to make in a short amount of time.

Lucky for you, I have compiled a list of tricks to help you avoid spending all your beer money on books.

- Try to buy your books from a friend (or stranger, whatever) who took the class before you.
- If your roommate is in the same class as you, see if you can share a textbook. This may or may not work, depending on your study schedule, how useful the book is, how early you both like to get your work done and how much you like your roommate. If you both have the same exam on the same day and you need the book to make sure you are doing the examples right— don't share a book (this applies to lots of economics, business, math and science courses). If the book is more of a reference and/or providing background information— think about it (might work for English, history, art history, music or poly sci).
- Obviously, try to buy used books over new. This is an easy one.
- Buy your books online. This can be a double-edged sword because you might end up waiting a long time for your books to come in (check where they are shipping from) which can be stressful. However, you will probably save a lot of money buying online instead of at a bookstore. Search by ISBN to make sure you have the right edition (this sometimes matters for doing the correct homework for problem sets but should not matter for most books), and buy early especially if you know you have to take the class and there is no chance of dropping it.
- If you have a question about any extras listed in the syllabus, email your professor to see how necessary the supplemental materials are before spending the money.
- Sell your old textbooks back. You can either do this at the bookstore (usually during finals week) or online. I haven't noticed much of a price difference between selling online

and selling at school, but sometimes the university bookstore won't buy back a certain book because the class isn't being offered again, and then you can sell the books online. You have to pay a small fee for shipping and you have to buy mailing envelopes.

- If you are trying to decide whether to rent or buy, use this rule of thumb: if the rental price is 30% of the used price of the book, rent! You probably wouldn't make more than that reselling your book anyway, and this way you won't get stuck with the book if there aren't buyers when you try to resell.

- If you are in a small program where everyone more or less takes the same classes, see if you can set up your own online marketplace. My small grad program (150 students) set up a googledoc where second years posted the books they had available, their contact emails and the prices they wanted for the books, and then new first years could email with offers. The spreadsheet was updated when the books were sold.

- ebooks— as a happy Kindle owner and ebook author, I love ebooks. However, I am not sold on e-textbooks (especially math and science books) because you often need to flip around in the book. Also, active reading (highlighting, taking notes in the margins) has been shown to increase comprehension. That being said, the price is usually better when you buy digital. Use your best judgment on this one.

- Don't forget your library! Your school library will probably have a copy of the book on reserve, and you can check it out for a few hours at a time (meaning, you can't go too far with it. Shucks.) This is great if you only need the book occasionally (check the syllabus) or if you suspect your professor is one of those inconsiderates mentioned above. Also, there is often one copy of the textbook in the stacks at the library. Snag it first thing in the semester and you can usually check it out for a few months at a time. Hopefully no one else will request it— but if they do, you usually have two weeks to return it which means you can order it online if you really need it. This is great if you aren't sure about staying in the class.

- My senior year of college I won a bookstore-sponsored scholarship. I got $500 worth of free books from the university bookstore for the year, which more than covered everything I needed (including notebooks!). Keep your eyes peeled for little pockets of scholarship money. $500 may not seem like a lot when applied to tuition, but not having to worry about paying for textbooks felt great.
- Remember one day you will never have to buy textbooks ever again!

Spring break!

Pollen's out, snow has melted, I spy a tulip...must be spring break season!

Everyone loves spring break. Warm weather, fruity mixed drinks, beaches, bikinis.... offers from your friends to go in on an "everything's included resort for just $, per person plus airfare" ...which, if you are like I was, you could never afford. How all those undergrads could pay for their jaunts to Europe and Thailand still puzzles me (they must have been trust fund babies and their peers who didn't understand credit card debt is not worth a week in Cabo).

Despite (still) never having been to Cabo, I managed to have a wonderful time on all of my post-legal-drinking-age spring breaks, and I never broke the bank. Here are some of the things I did instead— much more affordable and still loads of fun.

-One year I volunteered with a group to do post-hurricane construction work. The Gulf Coast is beautiful in the spring, I got to meet some great people at my university outside of my normal crowd, and we helped out people who really needed it. I have always enjoyed building/construction work, and putting on shingles in the sunshine with new friends was a welcome break from studying. Also, we were staying next to Brett Favre's bar on the beach, so we still had some traditional spring break fun!

-Nothing like a friend from Miami. One year my girlfriends and I drove down to Florida together, stayed at her mom's house, and took a side trip to the Keys. Her dad got us amazing tickets to a music festival and we had a great time. Lovely weather, live bands, home cooked food and only paying for two days of hotels= excellent vacation.

-I went to grad school in California, but during school I didn't have much time to explore parts of the West Coast that were father than a few hours away. One year my sister flew out to visit me and we explored southern California together on a road trip— Disneyland was our biggest splurge, but we also got a student deal on the San Diego Zoo. We stayed in hostels which I am officially too old to enjoy, used coupons for road trip fast food (I love McDonald's oatmeal, I don't care what anyone says), ate out of roadside stands and loaded up the car with snacks. We got to see a part of the country we otherwise wouldn't have had time to explore and we had a great time.

-My last spring break (sniff) I was still in California, and two of my girlfriends who were working across the country came out to visit me. We mainly stayed in my charming California city, where there was plenty to do— I got to play tour guide and we did the things I never had time to do when I was busy with school. We got Groupons for whale watching and went wine tasting in the middle of the day. We took a side trip out to the desert for a few days and stayed at a kitschy, dated spa.... aka, a really cheap, fun place. We paid for two nights at the spa hotel and the rest of the time we were able to cook and stay in my comfortable apartment. Even though I was still at home it felt like a vacation because I had friends visiting.

Some more general tips about vacationing on the cheap:

-Driving your own car instead of flying is usually cheaper. Especially with more than two people. Road trip!

-Airbnbs are great. Staying in an apartment means you can cook your own food, go to bed when you want, not stay in hostel dorms, and spend your money supporting an individual rather than a chain hotel.

- Any time you can avoid eating three meals out will save you a ton of money. Eating out for a whole week sounds nice, but I find it is expensive, I don't feel great after, I hate wasting the leftovers and I get tired of trying to find new places that are the right price and have interesting food. Try to get a hotel with a kitchenette (or free breakfast), if possible. Even if you just pack granola bars and fruit instead of paying for breakfast, you will save a lot of cash.

-I have a friend whose roommates saved all of their cans and bottles for the whole year then cashed them in. They made about $400, which made their road trip extra affordable. Other people save all of their change as their vacation fund— whatever works for you.

-Often times simple activities with friends (hiking, a day trip to a nearby town, bike rides, a picnic in the park, local camping) is more fun than an expensive trip. You can relax and enjoy the company without nagging guilt about how much you are spending. Spring break is timed so being outside is appealing again— take advantage!

The point is, there are lots of ways to have a wonderful time on spring break without breaking the bank. If all your friends are going somewhere you just can't afford, be honest with them. It might be that a few of them are in your same boat, and a lower cost vacation might be a better choice for them and you. Spring break is also a wonderful time to see friends who live in other parts of the country— think outside the box a little, and you will have a great time!

Takeaway actions and ideas:

- It pays to do a little research before signing up for student loans. Do your leg work and you will be in a much better financial situation when you graduate.
- This chapter includes some tips for getting textbooks on the cheap and also not blowing all your cash on one week of spring break.

Chapter 11: You work hard for the money: salary and raise negotiations and funemployment

The entire point of this book is for you to make the money you earn stretch as far as it can, so you can live the life you want to live. One of the best ways to do this is to make sure you are getting paid what you are worth at your job— here are some practical tips to make sure you're earning what you should be earning.

Salary negotiations

When you are offered a position, negotiating your salary before you start working is the single easiest way to earn more money at your job. Think of it as the world's most awkward ten minute conversation, but you can come out of it $5,000 richer. That is $500 per awkward minute.

When you are formally offered the job, the tables turn. You shift from being the "seller" to being the "buyer." Before, you were trying to sell yourself to the company. As soon as they agreed to hire you, things changed. Now you have the upper hand and you get to decide whether the salary, benefits and job are right for you. The best way to succeed at negotiating salary is to mentally shift your attitude. You should go from feeling like you are giving your number out to every man at the bar to feeling like every man at the bar is giving you his number (even if it's only one job offer. It's a simile.)

Reasons why it is important to negotiate your salary:

• You are confirming to your employer that you are as valuable an asset as they believe you are.
• The higher the salary you start with, the higher your earning potential in future jobs. If you stay in the same field, you should expect to increase your salary with

experience. If you start at a higher salary, you will make more throughout your life. Negotiating for an additional $5,000 early on could turn into $600,000 more in extra earnings throughout your career while doing the exact same work. C'mon.

- If you are worried about the company not being able to afford a few thousand, there won't be much job security at a company with such tight finances.
- You making more money reflects well on yourself, your education and your school (and your gender earning potential).
- And obviously.... you get more money for doing the same job you would be doing anyway.

But how do you negotiate for more money?

1. Do your research ahead of time. This means:

- Figure out the minimum you are able to survive on (while saving for retirement and emergencies. Don't forget to factor in income tax. You don't actually get to take home all the salary says you are getting.) Give yourself a little wiggle room. Do not accept less than this unless you want to be working two jobs or are able to reduce your expenses. Your dream job is not actually a dream job if you can't pay the rent while you are working there.
- Try to figure out a typical salary at the organization for someone with your same experience and job title (see if you can get location-specific information, as well). Check out online resources like LinkedIn and Glassdoor, and also look at the Opportunity Outlook Handbook, my favorite resource of all time.

2. Mentally prepare to ask for the high end of the range you have researched. Read some scripts to figure out what to say

without being awkward and uncomfortable. Do a mock negotiation with your mom or your dad or your roommate so you can ask for more money without squirming (I am serious. $5,000 or more is at stake!) Practice like you would practice a speech.

3. Try to put off the salary discussion until a job offer has been made in writing. If you can't manage this, that's ok. Just remember you're not actually hired until it's in writing and contracts are signed.

4. Wait until your employer says a number. If they insist you give a number first, give a wide (I'm talking $20k) reasonable range starting with your minimum. This should be based on your research.

5. Do not accept that number. Always go higher. Ask, "Is that your best offer?" Remember this is a negotiation so if you shoot higher than you actually want or expect you will end up where you want to be. Don't go crazy, but also do not undersell yourself— you don't look greedy, you look smart. They have already decided they want you and they expect you to negotiate. Show them you are really worth what they think you are worth. This will feel awkward (remember $500 a minute to feel squirmy), but you are basically doing another mini interview explaining again to them why you are worth what you (and they) think you are worth. Points to bring up again:

• Experience
• Education
• History of success
• Skills specific to this job
• Salary history
• Future potential for success at this job. What will you bring to the table?

- Industry salary averages (you did this research already, now ask for more than the average because you are an above average hire, right?)

6. Be polite, listen, ask questions, don't get upset and don't bring up personal reasons why you need more money. If you can't pay your bills with this job, it is not the right job for you.

7. If a higher salary is really not on the table, there are other things you can negotiate for. These things include:

- more vacation/sick days or even unpaid time off, if their vacation package is skimpy and/or you already have things planned. My good friend just got a job across the country and hasn't built up any vacation. In the next six months she has her sister's bridal shower, bachelorette party and wedding and she also has to go home to celebrate her grandparents' 60th wedding anniversary. She negotiated a for-six-months-only amount of unpaid time off so she can fulfill her family obligations.
- signing bonus
- paid moving expenses
- performance review with potential for a raise in 6-12 months (and subsequent reviews every 12 months after)
- end of year/performance bonus
- flexible work hours
- telecommute options
- parking/public transportation reimbursements
- see if your company will pay your student loans (your office may have a designated "professional education/development" pot of money they can tap into— it is worth asking to see if they can use that money to help

with your loans. This might be especially agreeable if you agree to stay on for a certain number of years.)
• other types of professional development, such as paying for conferences or classes
• stock options

8. Sometimes the answer will just be no. In this case, try to shoot for scheduling a performance review for future raises (you should be making approximately 2-3% more each year to keep up with inflation, so performance reviews should be standard). If you can't afford the job without a higher salary, walk away. Otherwise, take the job and the lessons learned during salary negotiations as an important life experience.

The point is, you will never know if you don't ask. The company wants you. If you don't have the conversation, you could be cheating yourself out of the easiest money you've ever made. Then sign up to make sure you get the full match on your 401k— the second easiest money you've ever made!

How to ask for a raise or promotion

If you're already in a job and are wondering how to bring up a raise and/or other benefits, here is a script you can write in an email:

> Dear Boss,
>
> Do you have any availability for a meeting in the next week or so? I would like to discuss some of my career goals and my contributions to this organization.
>
> Thank you,
>
> Me

Once you're on the calendar, make sure you have your pitch prepped. It's helpful to keep a running file of your achievements and responsibilities at your job so that you don't forget anything while you're talking about how valuable you are.

When you walk in to your meeting, here's how you can start the discussion:

> *You*: Thanks for meeting with me. I wanted to discuss some of my contributions to this organization and let you know I would like to be considered for a raise/promotion. As you know, I successfully did XYZ for the company this year, which is beyond what is listed in my job description. I have also done XYZ, which shows that I have been growing and providing value to the company. Here are XYZ things that I am planning to work on in the next six months that show even more growth. It is appropriate that my compensation reflects my high level of performance, which is why I would like a raise.

If your boss says a raise or promotion isn't on the table right now, push for another review in six months or a year. If it doesn't seem like you're going to get support to progress your career, it might be time to look for a new job. A new job offer can give you new opportunities for growth but it also can be used as a bargaining chip for a raise or promotion— especially if you can get a senior coworker to encourage management to keep you at your organization. It's best to wait until you have a job offer you are actually interested in just in case this tactic creates bad blood at work.

Advocate for yourself— find a mentor, be clear with your manager about your goals, and ask for what you want. Don't wait for people to notice your good work— make a list of all the contributions you have made and tell the people who should be paying attention. Get your managers on your side as coaches while you try to reach your work goals. The first time I did this, I was surprised at how receptive and helpful my manager was, but guess what? Supporting my career is part of his job! I thought promotions and raises were a thing I had to just wait and cross my fingers for, but when I told my manager my goals, he and I worked out a plan. I check in with him periodically with progress reports before my formal review cycles and we both have communicated how things are going. It feels good and I feel empowered.

How to be successfully funemployed

Job hunting is the worst. The actual worst. But this is what I know: It is going to be alright. How do I know? Because I have done this before. Remember? I graduated in 2008 and started job hunting exactly a week before the market crashed. Great timing, Kate.

Luckily, I had a roommate who worked as a gardener for a wonderful woman who ran her own garden design business. I was able to get a part time job gardening and I loved it. It was lovely to work outside, a great way to keep moving instead of sitting all day, extremely low stress and the worst thing that ever happened was a bee sting. My boss was a fantastic mentor and was extremely understanding, flexible, supportive and generous. Gardening was definitely not the prestigious job that I had expected for myself straight out of school, but it turned out to be a huge blessing that gave me the time and flexibility to think about what I really wanted to do next, rather than blindly apply to any job I could find.

Gardening for 15-20 hours a week was not quite enough to pay my bills and as winter rolled around our hours were reduced. I knew I had to look for other ways to supplement my income, because no one was hiring still.

One Friday afternoon, I was feeling really desperate. My bank account balance was frighteningly low. I was driving around the city, using up gas I could barely afford, asking all of the restaurants if they were hiring. I happened to drive by a temp agency and decided to see what kind of agency it was (I had no idea these things even existed, but they had the word "employment" on the sign). I walked in with my resume in hand, and I walked out with a two-day temp job writing Christmas cards for a company the very next week. I did a great job at my first placement and after that I had many more temp jobs, some of them relatively long term positions. Working for that temp agency helped to supplement my income, and I think walking in wearing professional clothes with my resume in hand is what got my foot in the door.

After a while, I started using some of my skills from academia. One of my freakish skills is I happen to be awesome at standardized tests. This had been useful twice in my life: once for the SATs and once for the GREs. I decided to cash in on my underused standardized test skills and I started tutoring the SATs a few hours a week. Each hour I tutored I was paid double what I was paid at my other jobs. It wasn't many hours, but it meant I could pay all of my bills and not have to worry about where next month's rent was coming from. I really liked working with the students and it was rewarding to see them succeed.

I was gardening, temping and tutoring— all while applying to jobs and internships— anything to get my foot in the door. As you can imagine, many months of applying for jobs and getting rejections, interviews and then rejections, or not hearing anything at all can be very depressing. Despite my three part time jobs, I still sometimes found myself with a lot of free time. After a few months without much happening on the job front, I decided I needed to shift my attitude. I wasn't unemployed, I was *funemployed*. Being funemployed means you look at the free time as a gift, a gift that helps you improve yourself.

I had lots of time to read, cultivate friendships, cook new meals, go to museums without the crowds, join a religious group, grow vegetables, stay out late at my friend's weeknight concerts, watch movies, exercise and take naps. I don't have time to do half of those things when I am working 40 hours a week, so I tried to spend a lot of time doing low-budget activities I enjoyed. Even though it was great to be able to do all of those things, it also was sometimes difficult when I had a week ahead of me with only 10 hours of work scheduled. I do better and I get more done with structure in my schedule— so I started volunteering on a regular basis for an organization that allowed me to practice my Spanish while also helping others— a win-win.

Finally, after nine months of being funemployed I got a job offer. The job offer was fantastic. At my new job, I made some of my best friends, learned a ton, and set the stage for grad school and eventually my future career. If I hadn't had that job when I did and if I hadn't worked with the people I worked with, my life would be very different today. Nine months of funemployment sounds terrible— but it wasn't all bad, and it led me to some wonderful things (including teaching me how to survive on not a lot of money, and now I can pass that information on to you!) In some ways, it was an amazing growing and learning experience.

Here is my advice for surviving funemployment:

- 90% of why you aren't hired doesn't have anything to do with you (especially if you have been successful in academia and in your past jobs). Put your best out there, but if someone else is an internal hire or has more experience or whatever...there is nothing you can do about it and it is not a reflection on you. It doesn't mean you did anything wrong (either in the application process or in life). There is just a lot of competition out there.
- Another dream job posting is right around the corner. Don't get your heart set on any one job. (This advice is also good for apartment hunting. And blind dates.)

- Add some structure to your days. Make yourself get out of the house at least once a day.
- I get more done the busier I am. Stay busy= apply to more jobs.
- Make plans with your friends, either during the day or at night. See your funemployed friends even more and commiserate together. It is super important you get out and aren't isolating yourself.
- Go see the touristy things in your town that are too crowded on the weekends.
- Find a volunteer opportunity that fits with your skills and interests. Try to make a regular schedule.
- Find a part time (or full time) temporary job that can help you stay afloat for a bit.
- Exercise every day. Set yourself a fitness goal that you otherwise might not have time to reach. You will feel better.
- Start a project! Learn to draw, make websites, start a blog, write a book, take photographs, organize your closets, start a garden, read a series of books, sew or knit or make candles, watch all of Hitchcock's movies. Whatever you want.
- Time to learn to cook! You'll save a ton of money and learn an important skill.
- Now would be a great time to get your financial goals organized.
- Join a club. Start a club! I love my book club.
- There is no such thing as a school night anymore. Check out some live weekday music or some late night happy hours.
- Visit family you don't normally have time to see.
- Networking is always cited as the key to successful job hunting. You can't network if you don't leave your house.

Look into professional societies and go to happy hours/volunteer events/public talks/free conferences.

- The best way to network is to ask people in your field for informational interviews over coffee. It'll cost you a cup of coffee, but it can be invaluable to learn from experts, and you alert them that you are capable, motivated and job hunting. I always find it flattering when people ask for informational interviews and I'm happy to give them (plus I love coffee). It's ok to use LinkedIn and ask strangers for career-related information— this is part of what LinkedIn is for.
- Take care of chores. Sometimes when you sit around all day the house can become a wreck without you even noticing. I like to do big piles of dishes first thing in the morning so I feel accomplished right off the bat.
- There are tons of free online courses and tutorials available. Are you looking at jobs that need a certain software skill set? Brush up (or learn) from YouTube, even if you don't own the software yourself.
- If you can afford it, now you have plenty of time to travel. Try to have internet access so you can keep job hunting.
- This is an awesome time for self improvement, whether it is professional or personal. Think about your bucket list and get to the less-expensive, more time-intensive tasks. Learn a language, join Toastmasters, start that novel.
- If you live with a partner, this can be a trying time for relationships. Try to channel some of your unfocused energy into doing loving things for your significant other. Also, if you are home all day and they are working, pay extra attention to doing the chores.
- Go for a hike on a Tuesday.
- Be nice to yourself. This is a difficult time, and it's ok if you occasionally spend eight hours watching Netflix marathons or sometimes feel sorry for yourself. Just remember—

when you are done being blue— think of this time as a gift and an opportunity— you are *funemployed*, after all.

It's going to be just fine. I promise.

Takeaway actions and ideas:

- Salary negotiation is the quickest, easiest way to make more money, so learn how to do it and do it well.
- If you're job hunting, hang in there. You're not unemployed, you're funemployed!

Chapter 12: Relationships and money

Your twenties and thirties are a time where many people have one or a few relationships. You might just be casually dating or you might be a decade into marriage, but all relationships require at least a little and sometimes a lot of money and financial planning. Feel free to skip around this chapter to whichever section applies to you right now.

Dating (for everyone interested in spending romantic time with another human)

I had a friend who stopped internet dating because he said he couldn't afford to take all those women out on dates. First of all, you shouldn't be eating a full meal with someone you meet online the first time you meet someone. You need a quick escape route without waiting for a server, a full meal is a big time commitment for a stranger who might be awful, and it legitimately does get expensive to eat out all the time. Coffee or drinks only for the first meeting, please.

Once you get over that awful phase of meeting everyone and you finally find someone you like, you want to wine and dine them and be wined and dined in turn. When you're broke, this can be tough—especially if your new squeeze has more money than you do but you still want to pull your weight in the fun activity department.

To date without breaking the budget, you have to get a little creative. The main thing that makes a successful date is a little planning— not spending. Here are some of my best suggestions for dating on the cheap. My husband calls these Kate Dates (if you just vomited in your mouth, I apologize. We can't help it.)

• Picnics are always a good idea! Go to your local park with a blanket (put down a shower curtain liner or a dry cleaning bag underneath if it's wet). Make some sandwiches, grab some sunscreen and some books, buy yourselves some sparkly lemonade or those individual wine boxes my family calls "juice boxes."

- Go for a hike or a bike ride. Pack a picnic!
- Check out community events. There are probably historical tours, guest speakers, interesting and/or funny museums, summer outdoor movies, festivals, free concerts, holiday parades. Everywhere I have ever lived (urban or rural— and I mean *rural*) had community events worth checking out.
- Speaking of museums, check for free admissions days or night openings. I know of a few museums that had jazz nights or cocktail hours in the evenings— not necessarily cheaper, but you get more bang for your buck when you get to hear music, drink wine and see art at the same time.
- Gallery openings have free wine, cheese, interesting art and interesting people.
- If you are a theater fanatic, see if you can volunteer to be an usher. Being an usher is more of a regular commitment, but you go early, help people to their seats or take tickets and get to watch a free show! This is a great way to see a large variety of performances. It doesn't necessarily mean you'll get to sit with your squeeze, but you've still watched a show together.
- Colleges and universities often have concerts, sports events and performances that are very affordable. No major league baseball in your area? Grab a bag of peanuts from the grocery and check out your college team. No college nearby? Check out your local high school teams.
- Hopefully one of you has a reasonably clean kitchen. Why don't you try learning a new recipe together? Have a frozen pizza on hand just in case.
- Watching movies at home becomes a lot more romantic if you planned a gourmet popcorn and a special cocktail for

the night. My favorite popcorn recipe: put olive oil in a smallish pot with a lid. Add salt. Let it get hot. Add popcorn kernels to cover the bottom of the pot and add some fresh or dried rosemary and salt. Cover and shake over high heat. Stop when the pot is full of popcorn (don't burn it! But if you do just start over.) There you go: incredibly impressive olive oil rosemary popcorn for about $.17 total.

- Spending too much on movies at home? Check out the selection at your local library.
- Make a string of dates around a theme, like "Finding the best donut in town." Sounds like multiple trips and multiple donuts...yum!
- Try to check out popular locations in the off season or play hooky on a weekday to avoid crowds.
- My family is full of board game fanatics. You know what is a fun date? Board game night! You can make your famous olive oil rosemary popcorn!
- Take a day trip to a nearby city you don't know very well. Be tourists!
- Actually, most people miss out on tourist attractions in their hometowns as well. Pretend you are moving in six months. What should you have done in the area that you just haven't gotten around to doing? Go do it!
- You know what is romantic? Stargazing. Especially if you have done your homework and know what's what up there.
- Bowling is usually pretty affordable and also pretty fun. Ditto darts or pool. A little friendly competition never hurt anyone (and if it does, dump him/her immediately. Life is too short to date someone who can't lose gracefully.)
- Pay attention to little perks you might pick up from your everyday life. Your work might offer free sports tickets or tickets at a discount. This year I got a four pack of major league baseball tickets for free because I bought jeans (that I was going to buy anyway, all I had to do was take a photo

of the receipt) and I also got a four pack of Steve Winwood tickets (I know, you are totally jealous) because I subscribe to the Sunday paper. Both of these events required me to do about three clicks worth of work with my phone, I don't get any spam mail because they are from two companies that I already buy from and the total value of the tickets was over $400. Awesome.

- Groupon and Living Social were invented so you can live like a manager on an entry-level salary.
- What if you volunteer together? Pick a cause you believe in or work you enjoy.

I'm sure you get the idea. To have a successful date you

1. need to like the person you are with and

2. need to do a little planning.

Other than that, you can wine and dine your squeeze without spending a lot of money, as long as you have spent a lot of thought!

A little note for anyone who is interested in having a wedding one day

Not everyone wants to get married, and not everyone who wants to get married wants to have a traditional wedding. Whatever floats your boat. But the fact is that a lot of people do get married and do want expensive weddings, and many people aren't financially prepared to pay for the wedding they want.

The median cost of a wedding is $18k. The number two reason for divorce is trouble with finances. If you start your marriage off with $18k of debt, you are starting your marriage off on rocky ground.

Now, I am not a wedding planning expert. I only planned my own wedding and we kept that pretty simple, but I do watch a lot of *Bridezillas* and *Say Yes to the Dress*. Weddings can quickly escalate to being out-of-control expensive, even if you are still keeping things simple. Part of this is because weddings are an industry designed to make you spend a lot of money (look into the history of wedding traditions, most traditions were invented to sell you things) and part of this is because it's just expensive to throw a large party. There are a few ways to pay for a wedding:

1. Your parents pay

2. Your partner's parents pay

3. Marry rich and your squeeze pays (word of warning: my mom says it is cheaper to borrow money than to marry for it)

4. Win the lottery

5. Start your married life off with lots of debt

6. Plan for it

I encourage strategy 6.

Strategies 1, 2 and 3 are all things that may reasonably happen, but as a full-fledged adult it isn't smart to expect the parents to foot the bill. So as an independent, financially savvy adult, you must *plan* for how to pay for your wedding!

Now, this may be less than appealing. Why would you start saving for your wedding when you might still be in the Tinder-induced "I wasn't sure whether to laugh, cry or run" phase of your dating life? Because you are smart. And you know $18k doesn't grow on trees. And one day you might want to have a wedding with an open bar. 80% of people get married by the age of 40, so statistically speaking, you will probably be one of those people. (No pressure, I'm just reporting facts here.)

Here is a hypothetical timeline:

Age 23: Go on date with man who tells you he used to have pet rabbits but he accidentally drowned them.* Swear off dating forever.

Age 25: Meet man who makes you laugh.

Age 25 and 6 months: Begin to suspect the man who makes you laugh might be the man you want to make you laugh forever.

Age 26: Get engaged.

Age 27: Get married. Have open bar at wedding.

When should you have started saving for this wedding? Well, it depends on the other factors in your life. If you are having trouble making rent, you need to focus on taking care of the basics. If you are taking care of paying your bills, paying off debt, building an emergency fund and saving for retirement and you still have some disposable income, then you can add saving for your wedding into your budget.

If you think one day you are going to get married it is wise to start planning financially. You might want to save on your own if you aren't sure about who exactly you are going to want to marry (this is very smart but it is not very smart to mention your wedding savings plan on a first date) or you might want to start saving as a couple. If you save as a couple you can each save $9k and take some of the pressure off. One benefit of a long engagement is you can use the time to

---

* Plural rabbits. True story. Yikes.

adjust your spending for a year or two to save up for your wedding.

The point is— you can take some steps now (regardless of your dating status) to give yourself a financial leg up in the happy marriage department. Starting married life without wedding debt is a wonderful gift to give to your partner and to your future self.

Things are getting a little more serious, I like this person a lot

When I was googling "How do couples manage their finances" to do a little background research, one of the suggested searches was "How do couples hold hands." That is sad. Let's stop googling it, people, and just give it a whirl. The worst that can happen is a little clamminess.

In my life, I hope to have a happy, functional relationship with clear communication and expectations. I am sure you hope for the same. However, a major reason for divorce is trouble with money and no wonder! Money is complicated, it comes with a lot of feelings attached, and people have different values and strategies and goals for dealing with money. Dealing with finances as individuals is tricky enough, let alone letting someone else into the mix.

Here is an example from when my husband and I were dating:

Hubs: My free subscription to XM radio should have ended yesterday [but the car still is playing XM]

Me: Make sure you aren't being auto billed for it. How much is it?

Hubs: About $6 a month.

Me: That is $72 a year! Are you going to cancel it?

Hubs: No.

Me: Seriously? You would pay $72 a year for XM radio? We don't even like any of the stations.

[Silence]

Me: Ok, I don't like any of the stations.

Hubs: Plus, there are no commercials. I think that is worth $72 a year.

See what happened there? We have different values and opinions when it comes to money and music and radio commercials. This was a tiny conversation, but every time we buy something out of the ordinary we are going to have to have a similar conversation (provided, of course, we are consulting our partners on our purchases). That is a lot of navigation to do! $72 a year really isn't a big deal, but this conversation was practice for future, bigger talks about money.

Here are some of the things that can add complexity to financial planning as a couple (mind boggling, really):

• One or both of you have kids. Maybe you have kids separately, maybe you have kids together. Maybe one of you has a kid from a former relationship. Who pays for what? Does your new spouse pay for the step kids? Even if it's the simplest situation (you each made half of each kid) it's still complicated.
• You might be committed but not married. How do you deal with buying property when you don't have the legal protection of marriage?
• One of you might make significantly more than the other.

- One of you might feel like it is your role to "provide," while the other partner may or may not agree.
- One of you might have huge amounts of debt. Is your partner expected to pay for the debt left over from your shoe splurge? Is that what partners do for each other when they love each other? Or is that your responsibility?
- One of you might stay home with the kids instead of working.
- You might think your partner buys stupid crap.
- One of you might come from money (please send me information on how you got that trust fund).
- One of you might want to go to school instead of continuing to work. Along those lines, one of you might want to switch careers to a more fulfilling but lower paying job.
- You might be a saver; your squeeze might be a spender.
- One of you might be much closer to retirement than the other or one of you may be much more financially prepared for retirement than the other.

You get the idea. Lots of pitfalls. But my general philosophy regarding finances is "Make a plan and try to stick to it." The only thing that makes couples finances different is it should be "Agree to a plan and try to stick to it and then communicate with each other."

But how do you structure a plan? What's fair? Here are a few examples of how other couples structure their finances:

Strategy 1: Dump it all together into one pot

In this strategy, you combine all finances and make sure all accounts are in both names (except federal student loans, please!*) The couple has one checking account, one savings

---

*This is because federal student loans taken out before marriage are forgiven if you die before your loans are paid

account, and share all credit accounts. All bills are paid out of this one pot.

Pros	Cons
What's simpler than having just one pot of money? It's very easy to keep track of your finances.	If you or your partner have different saving/spending priorities, this can be a recipe for conflict
If you make approximately the same amount of money and debt, this removes any hassle of splitting up bills and feels fair.	If one person brings in more money than the other, this can feel unfair.
If children or other complicated joint expenses come along, you never have to make decisions about who pays for what.	

Strategy 2: Keep it separate

In this system, each individual keeps their own bank accounts and their own credit accounts. Bills can be split down the middle or paid according to income levels (for example, if I make $100k a year and my husband makes $50k a year, I pay 2/3 of the bills and he pays 1/3).

off, so the spouse is not stuck paying for their dead partner's degree. If you add a name to your loan or consolidate, you lose this protection.

Pros	Cons
If you or your partner have different saving/spending priorities, this avoids fights over what the other spends money on.	If one person brings in more money or has more debt than the other, this can feel unfair and the lifestyles you each can afford may be drastically different.
This is most fair option mathematically.	You have to spend more time each month dividing up who owes what to pay the bills.
If you or your partner has bad credit, keeping assets separate can lower your interest rates.**	This system can get very complicated if you have children or if one person decides to go to school or change careers.
	It might be the fairest system mathematically, but in most relationships both individuals don't usually earn the same amount or work the same amount for the entire relationship.

Strategy 3: A little of both

In this system, all the money goes into joint accounts and all joint bills are paid out of joint accounts. Each individual has a separate, private checking account and every month they each get a set "allowance" automatically distributed into their private accounts.

** Keeping large joint purchases separate can mean that you pay lower interest rates but it also puts only one partner at risk in case you can't afford the purchase or in case of divorce.

Pros	Cons
If you or your partner have different saving/spending priorities, this avoids fights over individual purchases.	If one person brings in more money or has more debt than the other, this can feel unfair.
This is mathematically a pretty fair option.	You have to maintain at least three bank accounts.
If one partner has a lifestyle change, this system is already set up so no individual has to make a drastic change in spending habits unless it is a joint decision.	
There are never any questions about who pays for what.	

Like pretty much everything in personal finance, these guidelines only work if they are working for you. If your system isn't working for your relationship, try something else. The key things to remember are:

1. No one should feel taken advantage of
2. The system should be jointly agreed upon
3. The system can be changed if it isn't working

If you've tried all these systems and they aren't working, go see a professional couple's counselor. Financial troubles are common in marriage and professionals can help you figure out how to get on the same page.

Age gaps in marriage and strategic long term planning

It just so happens I married the world's best man who is 12 years older than I am. This means he will be eligible to tap into his retirement 12 years before I will, which means we can do some strategic planning now so we can access retirement money earlier if we choose to.

A few facts to set the stage: Roth style investments do not have any required withdrawals until you die. 401ks and 403bs require you start taking money out at age 70.5. You can start pulling money from any type of retirement account without paying extra fees at age 59.5.

I will be 59.5 in 2044, my husband will be 59.5 in 2032.

We have four tax incentivized accounts we can invest in, and we will always choose to build up our investments in this order:

1. His work account, using Roth-style taxation
2. His Roth IRA
3. My work account, using Roth-style taxation
4. My Roth IRA

We're choosing this investment prioritization because even though we want our retirement money to sit as long as possible so it can earn interest, we also want to have the option to pull money as early as possible (which is why we invest in my husband's accounts first). We also want to have the option to let it sit for a long time if we don't need it (one of a few reasons we choose the Roth-style tax system).

This means if we feel rich enough to retire early, we have penalty-free access to half of our retirement accounts 12 years earlier than if we invested in mine first.

The last thing you want to think about when you're newlyweds

I'm sorry to even bring this up, but it's prudent and I am a practical person. You and your partner should sit down and talk about your strategies for dealing with the three D's—death, divorce and disability. This means making sure your partner and kids won't be financially up a creek if you aren't able to work or aren't around anymore, and vice versa. Check into your life insurance policies, your disability policies, and think about prenups or even a postnup. These topics are awful, but showing your partner you want them to be cared for even if you're not there is an incredibly loving action.

Takeaway actions and ideas:

- There are lots of ways to impress your squeeze without breaking the bank.
- When you get into a serious relationship, talk about money and come up with a financial management plan as a couple.
- There are a few unfun topics (death, divorce and disability) that you and your partner should discuss and plan for in case the worst happens.

Bonus chapter: a few thoughts on wedding planning and planning other big parties

The biggest event most people will throw is a wedding, but much of this advice applies to any big party— a birthday, holiday or a random rager.

Planning a wedding without spending a gazillion dollars

This is not a wedding planning book, but it is a personal finance book and one of the hardest parts about weddings is you have to line up expectations (especially family expectations) with reality. Before spending money you might not have on printing off menus, matching shoes for bridesmaids, aisle flowers or favors, ask yourselves:

- Is this one of our priorities for our wedding day?
- Will anyone other than me/us notice if I skip this detail?
- Can we afford it?
- Does it have meaning for us?

If you said no to any of these, skip it with zero guilt.

The DIY trend and why it's probably not as savvy as it seems:

I love crafting. I refinish furniture, I've just taken up sewing, I'm a terrible but earnest knitter. In the world of Pinterest, you'd think I would love DIY-ing my wedding. Nope. We basically came down to two venues— one was cheaper but DIY heavy, and one was pricier but did everything for us.

We chose the non-DIY wedding and I cannot stress enough how incredible it was. Here's why:

- We lived across the country from our venue. My mom and my pregnant sister would have been on the hook to deal with all the local coordination. I love them and I did not want them to spend as much time on *my* wedding (aka, my responsibility) as I did. DIY= Do it YOURSELF, not asking other people to do things for you.
- It turns out even though I love weddings and I loved my wedding, I don't especially enjoy event planning. Coordinating schedules, keeping track of contracts, following through with vendors who don't call you back for weeks at a time (it happened a lot) ...to me that is *boring*. I didn't want to spend my time or energy doing it. Our venue did nearly everything for us.
- We didn't have to decorate! We chose a gorgeous church for our wedding and an art museum for our reception. Like I thought I was going to DIY better than actual artists? Forget it. And one less thing to worry about!
- We didn't have to worry about food or alcohol! While we did get sucked into the "you have to use our caterers with our venue" trap, it actually turned out to be just fine. Catering prices weren't far off from what was offered at the venue (plus I didn't have to coordinate). Our venue only offered heavy hors d'oeuvres and we added on a pasta bar so no one would be hungry— and it was great. Bonus: no one had to sit near anyone they didn't like during a formal dinner.
- I priced out the two venues and our non-DIY one ended up being about $3k more than the DIY venue (that's in total, including food and decorations and setup and renting equipment and lighting and linens and security and cleanup and liquor licenses and alcohol and bartenders and driving all over town all of these things I just did not care about and did not want to have to do). I did an estimate and I think DIYing all those extras would have cost about

$3k anyway, plus I would have had to coordinate labor and all of the tiny crappy details I didn't want to manage.
- The two things we did DIY were the invitations and the flowers. The invitations were super cheap to make, I thought they were cool and creative, but they took forever and I would never do it again.

Instructions for DIY invitations that will take forever: Buy confetti (which will arrive with leaves and sticks mixed into your giant, multi pound bag of confetti. Do not let the cat near the confetti bag.), glassine bags (those wax paper bags used to hold fast food cookies), envelopes and clear printable label paper. Print on the labels, cut them out, stick them on the glassine bags. Fill with confetti. Glue shut. Stuff envelopes, and ten hours later you and your fiancé will have sent out 150 wedding invitations. The invitations cost me maybe $35 in supplies, but was it worth the time? Nope.

My advice? Send an evite.

Skip what you don't care about

Here were my priorities for our wedding:

- get married
- have all of our family and friends there
- don't go into debt
- fried chicken for at least one meal
- have lots of toasts so people can say nice things about us

Here were my husband's priorities:

- get married
- have all our family and friends there
- have really good music
- open bar

So guess what! We had all those things. You don't need to have anything you don't care about at your wedding. Here are some things we didn't have (and I have not regretted for one moment):

- Expensive wedding bands. Mine was $30. My husband's was $150 but designed by a local artist. They look great. (Plus easily replaceable if your husband loses his at the gym. Not that that happened already, or anything....).
- Guest book. We got a ton of lovely cards anyway, and the best time to write mushy sentiments is not the time when there is a glass of champagne waiting.
- Engagement photos (if you don't have pictures of yourself in love yet, start snapping those selfies, kids!).
- Decorations (oh, you wanted something beyond the professional sculptors and painters whose work is at the art museum?).
- Limos (my beautiful pregnant-at-the-time-and-now-amazing-mom matron of honor was our designated driver and took us for a pit stop to McD's so we could fast fuel before the reception).
- Fancy rehearsal dinner. We had an uber casual one instead, in the (easy) beautifully refurbished hall at the church. We brought bubbly from Costco, beer and takeout fried chicken, and we ordered pies from the nearby local pie shop. It was exactly what I wanted. And delicious. My only regret was I didn't feel like I could eat the four pieces of fried chicken I actually wanted to eat, and instead only had two.
- Wedding cake. There is a local grocery chain that is famous for its cupcakes. At $.60 a pop, they were delicious and affordable and they looked beautiful. My husband and I cut a mini cake from a local bakery.

- Matchy bridesmaids. I asked them to pick their own navy dresses because I legitimately want them to have clothes they like and will rewear because they are my friends and I love them. If they showed up in green or black or red, I wouldn't have cared because my friends' presence is more important than my friends matching in pictures.
- Matchy groomsmen (they were never going to match anyway because had two different types of servicemembers in uniform and three civilians as groomsmen).
- Separate musicians for the wedding: the church has a world class organist which was included in the cost of the church, so we got to hear world class tunes!
- Formality. We didn't even have the sit down dinner option available to us. My dad called after the wedding and raved about how much he loved being able to spend the reception time catching up with exactly the people he wanted to see. Our friends and family are pretty spread out, so it was nice that people could treat our wedding as a mini reunion.
- "Wedding" save the dates. We ordered our own postcards from an online printing company and we chose the "business" postcards instead of the "save the date" postcards. The business option was half the cost, looked exactly the same and we could use postcard stamps instead of letter stamps, which saved us even more.
- A full photographer's package— we didn't want the photo album or the engagement photos and saved a few hundred dollars just by asking to have fewer "add ons."
- Fancy flowers. I didn't really care about flowers and ordered mine in bulk from Costco. I cheaped out and ordered less than I should have and it showed, and I wish I had just skipped them because I just didn't care about them! Plus I had to have my amazing bridesmaids make the bouquets at the last minute because they didn't arrive looking like I expected. This violated my DIY-means-don't-

ask-other-people-to-do-work-for-me rule. I am sorry and thank you. Also, Goodwill is usually a treasure trove of matching vases, so go there before you buy new ones.

Be a little bit extravagant (but don't go crazy)

Remember how one of my priorities was to not spend too much on this wedding? While many brides go overboard, I am inclined to go underboard (see: flowers). Things I could have skipped but am glad I didn't:

- A bus to keep my guests safe. The bus drove guests from the hotel to the church, to the venue with the open bar and then back to the hotel. I didn't have to worry about any of my closest friends or family members drinking and driving. I cannot think of anything more devastating for a newly married couple than having someone get injured on the way home from the wedding. I was quoted prices between $700 and $4,000 for a bus, so do some shopping around before you commit.
- Favors. I hate going home with one engraved wine glass that doesn't match anything else in my house. I feel like almost all wedding favors end up in the landfill and are a huge waste of money and time and energy. I do, however, like favors you can eat. We found a woman who makes her own chocolates, and she put together mini boxes of artisan chocolates for us. We supported a local business owner, and favors aren't for the bride and groom anyway, so even though I don't really care about favors it was a good purchase.
- The dress. Ok, I wouldn't have skipped wearing a nice dress. Since I am a military spouse, I qualified for a free dress from Brides Across America. I felt kind of weird about taking a free dress, because my husband is mid-

career and I have a career of my own, so we could afford a wedding dress. They only have events twice a year, and my sister was in town, so we decided to go anyway just to see. We found a dress and it was fine. It was a C+ dress. It didn't quite fit, it wasn't quite my style…. but wedding dresses are so expensive and ridiculous for just one day, I figured I would make it work. I got it altered at the place I got it from, but the alterations took it from a C+ to a D+. Plus, it still didn't fit. So instead of spending $300-$500 to fix a dress I didn't really like, my mom and I went to a bridal salon that was going out of business and got a dress I really liked. It wasn't a bargain, but it also wasn't full price. I loved it. The non-fitting dress went back to Brides Across America for someone with a different body shape.

- Hair/makeup/nails and henna (my husband is half Indian so we pulled in some of his cultural traditions). I thought I was going to do my own makeup, but who are we kidding, I can barely put on mascara. Plus it was great to spend time with all my bridesmaids at the same time, and the henna was gorgeous.

The dress

Here are some things that make wedding dress shopping hard:

- Wedding dresses are obscenely expensive and you are wearing it one time. Once. In a cost per hour analysis, you're not doing so hot. That makes you feel like you have to find a dress you loooooooooooooooooove. I don't know about you, but I have a hard time finding $30 plain cotton sweaters I even like a little bit. Shopping is hard.
- I love the Friday night *Say Yes to the Dress* binge as much as the next girl, but that show makes it hard to go wedding

dress shopping without ridiculous expectations that you are supposed to find "the one" out of the millions of dresses that are produced and marketed to be sold to you.

- Wedding dresses are like your future spouse— you love him/her, you're glad you found him/her, but there are seven billion people in this world. Statistically speaking, there are going to be other humans out there who have similar values/personalities/physical traits/upbringings as your future spouse, and you would probably have a happy marriage to a different one or a hundred or a thousand of those other human beings who are similar to your spouse. (I'm not the romantic in my marriage, can you tell? Realism, guys. Realism.) Dresses are the same. There is not just one dress that will make you happy. There are multiple dresses that will make you happy.

- A good lesson from *Say Yes to the Dress*, though? Don't even try on anything you can't afford. Everyone has a budget, so know yours before you even think about walking into a store.

- After you buy it, chances are you will need another few hundred for alterations. Just in case it wasn't expensive enough.

- I loved my dress. Loved it. But even I had mixed feelings about it before my actual wedding day. I didn't have the *"this is the one"* moment. Because that's what happens on TV. This is real life and it's ok to not have TV feelings about clothing choices. Choose something within your price range you are comfortable in and you feel pretty in. That's it. That's the secret to finding the dress that is "the one."

I learned a few tricks about places to get less expensive wedding dresses.

- So many bridesmaid dresses come in white! No one will ever know.
- There are a few charities that will take wedding dresses (note for after the wedding) and resell them at a discounted price.
- This newfangled thing called the interwebs sometimes has good deals.
- Borrow a friend's/family member's dress.
- Target?!?! sells wedding dresses. I am not kidding. Walmart does not. I checked.
- Other less traditional places: ModCloth and BHLDN (part of Anthropologie).
- Pastel wedding dresses are in, and I for one love the trend. You know what else is in? Pastel prom dresses. Just flip on some K-Ci & JoJo and head back to the ole prom dress section of the department store.

Last note— try to get some free champagne when you are shopping. I went to multiple shops and not one glass was poured. Wah waaah. Guess that's what happens when you wedding dress shop at Target.

Takeaway actions and ideas:

- Don't go into debt for your wedding.
- You can skip a lot of wedding "things" and still have an amazing celebration that fits in your budget.
- Wedding dress shopping is not like on TV.
- Don't worry about whether things will go wrong. Things will go wrong. Things have gone wrong at every wedding from the beginning of time. It doesn't matter. None of the usual stuff that drives couples crazy is really that important. Only one thing matters: that the couple have a wonderful time. That's it.

Chapter 13: For the ladies

Gender wage gap

In case you did not know, ladies, we make $0.77 for every $1.00 a man makes doing the exact same job. There are some factors that skew this data a bit (like taking time off to have babies and an imbalance between male and female engineers)— but if you have the same skills and background and are doing the exact same job as a man, you should be making the exact same amount as that man is. Time to move society forward, people. Women are badass and it is time we get paid for it.

One of the reasons people say women make less than men is their reluctance to negotiate for more money. Do you have the same experience, education and skills as that man over there? Then you should be making the same amount of money. Period. So think about all of the awkward crap women have to deal with in their lives—annual appointments, running into ex-boyfriends, bikini waxes— all much worse than talking with your boss about how valuable you are and why your pay should reflect what you are worth. $500 per awkward minute. You can do it! Go read chapter 11 again, throw your shoulders back and develop a solid pitch. The work you put in now will pay off for you, for your family, and for future women in the workforce.

Money and being a mama

There are so many parts of parenthood that are going to rock your world in both amazing and not so amazing ways (baby giggles come with poosplosions), and one of these parts is money. It's no surprise kids are expensive— and those expenses start with a reduction of income.

The Family Medical Leave Act (FMLA) protects your job for up to twelve weeks while you're out on maternity leave. This doesn't mean you'll get paid anything at all. Your job might offer maternity leave benefits, it might offer partial benefits, you might have to apply for short term disability, or you might not get any income. When you decide to start trying or when you find out you're expecting, it's a good idea to spend some time readjusting your finances so you take into account the income you might be missing out on while you're recovering and bonding with your new nugget. Also, don't be surprised if giving birth leaves you with a hefty hospital bill even with insurance, so do a little research about average costs and try to save up before your nugget arrives.

Your partner may or may not receive paid paternity leave, and if you are in a same-sex relationship you may face even more hurdles getting bonding time with your baby. Take any income shortages for your partner into account, too. If you don't like how maternity leave is structured in America, call your representatives and vote.

There are a ton of resources out there to help you save money as a parent, so here are my tiny tidbits of advice:

• There are so many baby clothes in the world that we will never, ever run out. Instead of buying new, ask for hand-me-downs or check out consignment shops. Babies grow so quickly that a brand new outfit can be worn maybe ten times before it's out of rotation, so most baby clothes have very little wear and tear.
• You need a lot fewer clothes than you think you do. Depending on your laundry and spit up situation, I would recommend no more than fourteen outfits for any size—less if you have a washer and dryer in your home.
• That being said, if you have overexcited grandparents buying tons of baby clothes whether you want them to or not, ask them for a variety of sizes through 18 months. Most new parents end up with 70% newborn clothes that

their baby outgrows within a few weeks and then have to stock up on other sizes.

- Babies develop so quickly that the majority of baby products are barely used. You can save a ton of money by buying basically everything baby related used— just check for recalls. The exceptions here are car seats and cribs, which you should not buy used for safety reasons.

Going back to work...or not

Many parents look at the cost of childcare (a thousand or more a month) and decide it isn't financially worth it for one parent to keep working. There are a number of reasons why people decide to become stay at home moms or dads, but women face more pressure to stay home because of lower wages overall (see: stupid gender wage gap), breastfeeding and cultural norms. To make things worse, the motherhood wage gap means mothers make $.71 for every $1.00 a father makes. If you choose to go back to work, keep this additional financial penalty in mind and be even more prepared to negotiate for raises during performance reviews.

Speaking of breastfeeding, you are legally supposed to have the time and a private space (not a bathroom stall) to pump while you are nursing. Despite what the breastfeeding pamphlets you got at the hospital might say, this may not be feasible in jobs such as teaching, waitressing, construction, any job with a lot of travel or office jobs with open floorplans. The law lags behind practical constraints when it comes to working mothers who pump or breastfeed, so come up with a plan before you return to work.

How to save money while dealing with your period and other fun topics

Periods are the worst, right? Ugh. Tampons and pads are expensive and they make a lot of waste. Plastic applicators will be around forever. To make things worse, tampons will cost you about $50 a year. You'll probably have your period for around 30 years. That's $1,500 in tampons in your lifetime. $1500 you are flushing down the toilet while dealing with accursed periods. Note: while getting pregnant will reduce your tampon costs, it is more expensive in every single other respect.

A menstrual cup and reusable pads are not for everyone, but they are most definitely the affordable life choice to deal with your period. A quality menstrual cup costs around $30 and can last between from two to five years— if you only used menstrual cups, that's about $300 for a lifetime of period needs. If you use reusable pads, you can take care of your period for life for $200. Think about ditching the disposables and make your period a little less financially and environmentally burdensome.

Speaking of pregnancy being expensive— at some point in your life you will probably take a pregnancy test. Pregnancy tests are $8 a pop at the drugstore and $1 each at the dollar store. Being pregnant is a yes or no thing so even if you're not sure you trust the dollar store test (although they work just fine) you can check the results eight times over and by then you should be very well hydrated and have a clear answer.

1-800-799-7233

The number above is the National Domestic Abuse Hotline. Domestic abuse is not just physical or emotional, it can also be financial. If your partner controls the money, limits your ability to get or hold a job, prevents your access to credit or runs up debt in your name, you may be a victim of financial abuse. (Sticking to a budget and limiting household spending you have agreed upon isn't financial abuse. If you disagree about a budget, it's time to make a new budget.)

Financial abusers often intentionally make women believe they don't have enough money to survive on their own as a tactic to control them and to prevent them from leaving. If you are in an abusive relationship and fear that you won't have enough money to survive is keeping you from leaving, here are some things you should know:

1. Professional victim advocates see this all the time and have resources to help you. You're not alone.
2. There are safe places for you and your children and even your pets to go, both short term and long term.
3. There are legal and financial services that can help you get back on your feet.

If you need help, it's just a phone call away. If you want to hear a story that will give you some hope and perspective, check out Dax Shepard's *Armchair Expert* podcast in which he interviews his mom, Laura Labo (aired July 2, 2018).

You are not alone. Everything that's worrying you financially is temporary and fixable.

Takeaway actions and ideas:

- The wage gap is real, but you can advocate for yourself to earn what you deserve. Be brave, it's important.
- Becoming a mom comes with a bunch of new financial choices— consider your values as well as your value.
- Periods can be cheaper if you use reusable products.
- There is help for financial abuse. If you need it, use it.

Chapter 14: Money, the world and you

How I spend my money has an impact on the local economy, the nation's economy and the global economy. The economy impacts a lot of people's daily lives, so paying attention to your money and how you spend it is part of being a good human being. You, as a consumer, have the ability to vote with your dollar. You can choose to spend your money to support the things that are important to you, and you can choose not to spend money on things you don't want to encourage in the world.

The power of your money— or, voting with your dollar

Here is my confession up front: I try to be a conscious consumer, but sometimes sales are too good, my budget is too tight, I don't have the time or I just plain want something that isn't in line with my higher values.

Do you worry about plastics in the ocean and overflowing landfills? Shop for used goods and try to buy in bulk packaging. Reduce your consumption and your waste.

Worried about the economy or international labor practices or the carbon footprint of transporting stuff across the world? Buy used goods from your neighbors or from a local charity, or only buy items made in America.

Care about the arts? Buy art from local artists instead of from big box stores.

Think about the things you care about and the way you want the world to look, and then spend your money in a way that supports your worldview. When I was finishing grad school, I had a friend who was frustrated that the program we had finished did not put enough emphasis on her field of specialization. To encourage the program to change, she

173

decided to donate money to a program that was specifically earmarked to fund resources needed for her specialization with a letter explaining that she thought her specialization needed more resourcing. Do you think the administration cares more about a frustrated student heading out the door, or a long term donor's suggestion for change? Putting some cash behind your complaints may feel counterintuitive, but it can affect the change you want to see.

The bottom line: when you spend your money, some influence travels with that dollar. Maybe you don't have a lot of money— but if you have any at all, you still have monetary influence. So be aware of what you are spending on, and try to make purchases that support the things that are important to you.

Managing your stuff

If you're like me, you once bought a sweater online. Then you got emails twice a day for the rest of your life trying to sell you more sweaters. Most days it doesn't work, but occasionally you think, "You know what? I could use a new sweater." So occasionally you buy a new sweater.

Shopping feels good, buying new things feels good, thinking you've gotten a great deal feels good, feeling like you have enough clothes in case you lose your job and can't buy new ones feels good. All of these things feel good.

But.

Debt feels bad, clutter feels bad and waste feels bad. Shopping too much is not sustainable for your wallet, your home, or your lifestyle. Multiply that sweater email times 1,000 and that's the pressure we have every day to buy new stuff. It's how the economy runs and it keeps people in jobs (often actually not in working conditions we would support if we could see them), but it's also expensive, wasteful, excessive and exhausting, and you end up with a closet full of

45 sweaters despite the fact that you ignored 99% of those emails.

Here are a few thoughts for how to deal with buying (or not buying) stuff.

My family moves a lot, and we have very high limits on the amount of things we are allowed to pack into those moving trucks. This means we don't have any incentive to clean out our stuff, and when we get to a new house we often have to spend a lot of time rearranging and buying new stuff to fit the new space. You can imagine this gets old, fast.

For a number of reasons, my family ended up moving into a ginormous McMansion with more bedrooms, bathrooms and floor space than we need or want. Do you know how much time and energy I have spent organizing all of our crap and then *keeping it clean*? (I hate cleaning. Not my best skill.) I always prided myself in not owning a lot of things and not being especially driven by materialism, but somewhere along the line I discovered that we own three air mattresses and four full sets of coasters. I don't ever want to host that kind of party, so why have we been hauling this stuff around?

One day I was feeling frustrated that I kept having to reorganize my closet and I realized if I didn't own so much stuff, I wouldn't have to manage it.

That was a big breakthrough for me, so let me say it again: *if I didn't own so much stuff, I wouldn't have to manage it.*

I decided to start clearing out our crap, and I am both embarrassed and astounded at what we have. Now, I think it might take a certain mindset to be ready to clear out your things and to stop buying stuff, because I too cracked Marie Kondo's book (you know the one, where you only keep things that "spark joy") but I didn't make it past the first chapter because it was making me feel guilty and anxious and I didn't want to confront the fact that I enjoy shopping for things I don't need and I really, really enjoy feeling like I got a great deal.

I am still struggling with this last issue, but somehow as I began clearing things out I found I did not want to fill up those empty spaces. I also realized I buy lots of things because the price is right and I hope I will end up liking them, instead of waiting to buy the thing that will work perfectly for me. This realization has made it a lot easier for me to say no to the bargain item that might or might not be what I am really looking for.

The more crap I clear out, the more satisfaction I get. I thought it would be hard— and for some things, it is hard. But for other things, it's been incredibly easy and actually very fun. Here are some things I have been thinking/learning about/doing:

- Capsule wardrobes. There are people all over the internet who have figured out exactly how many items of clothing you need to reasonably get dressed. You're actually probably already doing this, because if you're like me you regularly wear about 30% of your clothes and the other 70% you can't get rid of because you say, "But what will I wear if I get rid of that?" The answer, of course is, "You will wear what you currently are wearing, doofus, because you don't actually wear that." I like to look very professional for my day job and I used to spend a few hundred every season to "refresh" my clothes. Of course, I wear a few items a lot, but the majority of my new purchases aren't quite right and end up sitting in my closet. Turns out, I don't actually have to spend $200 quarterly to look great and fresh, I just need some strategic planning and quality items.
- Selling your stuff. I have made over $750 this year selling our crap on Facebook marketplace. It is easier than Craigslist but still a hassle to meet up with buyers. That being said, $750 and a sense of accomplishment is pretty great and worth it.

- Planning carefully when we go into stores and possibly avoiding stores altogether. We went to Target (the Temple of Temptation) the other day because we needed some baby proofing gear. That's all we needed. There weren't any carts available, so I got a basket. Between managing the baby and only carrying a basket, guess what we bought from the store where I want to buy everything? Baby proofing gear, eggs, and a hard-to-find cocktail mix. Whatever, we're only human.
- Curating. My older sister designs commercial products and is extremely good at choosing the correct item for the purpose she wants. Once she spent a whole weekend looking for the perfect teakettle. I'm not very good at envisioning the perfect item and I'm also a sucker for a good deal, so I end up with four items that kind of work instead of one item that is perfect (note: this is not actually saving money). My teakettle's handle burns my hand when it heats up and my sister's teakettle is perfect. I am trying to be more like my sister and less content with abundant mediocrity. This goal is also helping me focus on replacing five duplicate crappy items with one that actually works.
- The right numbers of household goods. You know what else the internet has? Lists of how many of each household item we should have. We had over *thirty* old bath towels in my house. The ones in the best shape were mine from college years, and we don't have a single matching set for company. Guess what? The internet told me we should have three matching towel sets for every person in our house. We need six nice towel sets, not thirty embarrassing old ones. If you're making a wedding registry, look up one of these lists instead of inventing your own numbers.

Here are some things you might get hung up on:

- The original cost of the item: *at this very moment,* I am selling a nearly new clothes steamer for $20, and it retails new for $90. I feel like I'm maybe not getting the best deal I could get and I almost don't want to sell it for $20. However. We own an iron and an ironing board. We have never used the steamer. This item is completely superfluous. We are paying to keep it in our house by thinking we "need" a big place and then paying rent for it, when in reality we could be fine with half the stuff and half the floorspace (and half the rent). Is this steamer worth more than $20? Sure. Do I wish I could do better reselling it? Sure. But realistically, your old stuff is not worth even half of what you paid, so chalk it up to experience and be very careful what you buy going forward.

- Meeeeeeeemmmmmmmmmories. I had *three boxes* of notes from high school I have never, ever gone through. I have been carrying these boxes around for fifteen years, shipped them across the country three times, and didn't even care enough about them to look at them once in fifteen years. I finally made myself go through them and while I found some gems (letters from my Gramma, a note from a friend telling me she really enjoyed getting pretzels with me) I also found things like:
  - A construction paper star with my name on it
  - Blank postcards
  - Rusty pins made out of potato chip bags
  - Three broken plastic bead bracelets

These things had been taking up space and energy and gas to cart it across the country for fifteen years. Time to move along. I bought myself and my husband one plastic bin each and that is the space we are allowed to use for items we want to keep to remember. That's it.

- Shopping for fun. This is a tough one. Here are a few ways I've allowed myself to scratch that itch without actually going crazy:
  - Let yourself bargain hunt at the grocery store. Stay within budget, but if you see a food you really like for a great deal, stray from your list a little. A box of cookies is $3 and will be consumed while a sweater would have been $30 and will take up shelf space. Just don't buy anything you won't eat.

- Go to the library. I'm a big reader and it feels like treasure hunting when you can find the book you were looking for. Plus, free!
- Go shopping, but channel my sister. Have a specific item in mind and then only buy it if it is perfect (including perfectly priced). Do not get a large cart at the store.
- Go shopping, but stick to a tight budget. Want to spend a day at the outlets? Fine! Take cash out of the ATM and only spend that. Save your receipts and return anything that isn't perfect or you haven't used within three weeks.
- A tight budget is also a great way to enjoy farmer's markets or bulk stores, (helloooooo samples). It is easy to overspend at both of these places, so again, cash is the way to go.
- Consignment or thrift shop. This might backfire in terms of lowering the amount of stuff you have, but the prices are usually right and if you enjoy treasure hunting this might be the strategy for you.

- Bargains. You remember how I don't actually wear 70% of my wardrobe? The majority of items I don't wear were purchased because they were pretty okay and because they were on sale. Spending $20 on a shirt that was originally $100 is still a waste of $20 if I never wear the shirt.
- Gifts. Gifts are tough because they come with a nice heaping side of emotional baggage. Unless the gift is a family heirloom, there shouldn't be strings attached to gifts. Once it's yours, do what you want with it. It was wonderful the giver thought of you, you said thank you and hopefully wrote a note, but now it's yours to return, regift, or give away. You do not have to keep it.
- Things from people who have died. (Let's just keep piling on emotional baggage.) I try to think about what my loved one would have wanted in relation to their stuff. When my gramma died, she had two full sets of china. I grew up eating off one of the sets, so I was happy to take it. I use it and I will keep using it rather than storing it as an

untouchable item, because my gramma used it and she would never want me to feel burdened by her things. If I break a dish, I'll have broken it while I was using it and remembering my gramma instead of keeping it locked away in storage for no reason.

When I was unpacking the things I got from my gramma's house, I ended up with a framed drawing I had no memory of. I felt badly about getting rid of it, but I know my gramma wouldn't have wanted me carrying around a random drawing out of guilt for the rest of my life. I'm happy to have and love the items of hers that have meaning, okay with letting go of the things that don't.

- Your partner's stuff. My best advice here is: it's a marathon, not a sprint. Be respectful and remember people are more important than either keeping or getting rid of things. Don't be a hoarder. If you're dating a hoarder make sure he or she gets therapy before you move in and not after. It might take years, but you'll figure how to manage your belongings as a couple.

Some of this advice goes a little bit beyond dealing with finances, but the fact is the amount of stuff you own will have a direct effect on your money. If you have less stuff, you'll have more money, need less square footage and therefore can pay less on rent (or, gulp, storage units to store your crap), have less to manage and less to clean. Getting rid of your stuff can make you a little bit richer if you sell it or donate it (save your receipts, tax deductions!). In the long run, think about the type of life you want— do you want more things or more experiences? Do you want a few quality items or a lot of bargain items? Choose the lifestyle you're interested in, and then adjust your shopping habits to reflect what you want.

Giving back

"I've made all my money on my own without my family and I work very hard." —Paris Hilton

Unless you are Paris Hilton, you probably owe some thanks to other people for helping you get to where you are today. Your schools probably helped you out quite a bit (I know you can read, so that is something to be thankful for). Maybe you had a life changing experience at a summer camp. Maybe you find your fulfillment playing a sport and you'd like others to play too. Maybe you or someone in your family had an illness you would like to help find a cure for. Maybe your rescue dog is your best friend.

The point is, we all have had things in our lives that have been important in some way or another, and most of us didn't get here on our own (except for Paris Hilton, obvi). That is why it is important to give back.

Considering all of the other financial obligations you are facing for the first time, giving back can be very daunting in your twenties. If you are a student with loans, you are probably very aware every dollar you spend now will cost you more in the future, so this may not be the time for you to make monetary donations. This does not mean there aren't ways for you to give back, they just might not be financial at this time in your life.

If you are paying off loans or other debt, you are probably also very aware the money you put towards your debt today will save you money in the long term. It can be easy (and tempting) to put off making financial donations until you are debt free.

...but you might buy a car. Or a house. Or start a business. Or have kids and send them to college. As we get older, most people make larger purchases that require they go into some sort of debt. Chances are, you will have some sort of debt in the future. And as we already discussed, you didn't get to the point where you can buy a house without benefiting from education, the love of your loyal rescue dog, etc. etc. So being in debt is not a good excuse not to give back (but don't go into debt because you give more than you can afford. That isn't helping anyone either.)

If you have any sort of disposable income at all (this means you can pay all of your required bills on time without going into debt— and no, paying for beer does not count as a necessary expense!), you can afford to give some cash back to your community.

How do you decide how much to give? Christian tradition supports tithing, which is 10% of your income. Other people give suggested donations depending on what the charity asks for. Other people have a certain amount scheduled into their budgets and then distribute to each of their favored charities using automatic bill pay (don't be surprised this is my method of choice). I especially like to donate on match days.

If you don't feel you can make financial donations right now (or if you are a student living on loans), consider volunteering your time. There are always opportunities to help out your community, and many would argue a gift of time is more valuable than a gift of money. You can work for a formal volunteer organization, organize a drive, or fundraise to run a race. There are tons of options.

Giving back is personal— what you choose to give (time, money, talent), how much you choose to give, who you choose to give to. But I hope you will choose to include charitable donations as part of your budget and as part of your lifestyle— part of growing up is recognizing those who have helped you get to where you are today and giving back to your community (I'm talking to you, Paris).

Keeping up with the Joneses

We have some friends who seem to have an amazing life. They both own luxury cars, they have a vacation house somewhere warm (and fly there all the time. Like every other weekend.) Facebook makes them look like they are doing very well. I am sure you have similar friends— they travel all the time to amazing places (how do they get the vacation days?? That is my biggest question!) and they have great clothes and great cars and maybe they just bought a house and you are still renting with three roommates.... You wonder how they got there and why you aren't there yet, and maybe you are jealous and you wonder what you did wrong.

I have some things to say about this.

There are a few ways they could have gotten there, and many reasons why you should not compare your circumstances to their circumstances.

1. Maybe they come from money and their family resources allow them to live like this. Do you have a wealthy family who gives you money to travel or buy houses or fancy cars? Me neither. I didn't do anything wrong, and my friends aren't more successful at life than I am. They just come from a wealthier family.

2. Or maybe they are super successful at their jobs and can afford it. Good for them! That is awesome and you should be thrilled if your friends have sweet gigs they enjoy. If they don't enjoy their jobs, well, then they'll hate their jobs and carry on, or maybe they'll switch to different jobs which might or might not allow them to maintain their lifestyle. Everyone who works, whatever their income level, deals with these questions.

3. Or maybe they're in debt. Do you know what their finances look like? I *could* buy a Porsche right now if I went into debt to buy it. I just don't want to have to make those payments every month, because there are other things I want my money to go to and you know how much I hate paying interest. This is a choice I am very happy with, but other

people might want the Porsche enough that the debt would be worth it.

4. Or maybe they can afford it today and they aren't planning for tomorrow. Maybe they have a vacation house on the beach but no emergency fund, no retirement savings, and no spare money for other savings goals. Everyone makes different financial choices. I'd rather have a worry-free retirement tomorrow than a fancy lifestyle today. But that's just me.

So think about those friends who have it all. Do you know which category they're in? Probably you don't. You might think they come from family money, but maybe they are in debt. Maybe you thought they were loaded because they have good jobs, but maybe they inherited a big chunk of money. Keeping up with the Joneses is a tough trap to fall into, and it is harder to remember *you* make your financial choices based on *your life*. Just remember, you never know what other people's bank accounts look like, no matter what kind of car they drive.

Conclusion

That's it! That's the whole thing. I hope this book has made you feel more confident about your financial choices, and I hope it has paved the way for your life goals. Remember that exercise we did in chapter one, where you had to list your feelings about money? No matter how much money you have, you can manage your resources so that you only have positive feelings about money. You do not have to be intimidated, stressed or overwhelmed by your finances.

This book is a jumping off point to get you set on a good trajectory for your working years, but it's not the only resource out there. If you want to learn more about investing, advanced retirement savings, taxes, how to retire early— whatever! — there are lots of resources. Hopefully you have realized financial management isn't as complicated as it is portrayed, and if you made it through this book you certainly have the skills to manage your own finances into the future.

You only have so much time and energy in your lifetime, and you now know how to make the most of your money so you can spend your time and energy on the other things you want to do. Confronting financial challenges head on, creating systems that work for you, and making your money work to support your goals will lead you to a better quality of life for you, your partner, and your family. That's the whole point of money— so make a financial plan that works for you, and go enjoy your life.

If you have questions, feel free to email twentiesinyourpocket@gmail.com. You can also check out my blog, www.twentiesinyourpocket.com, or look up Twenties in Your Pocket on Facebook.

Acknowledgements

Thank you to the incredible group of people who helped me write, edit, design and publish this book. A special thank you to Lucy Alejos, Gerard Gonzales, Jonathan Scheller. A huge thank you to Jolenta Greenberg and Kristen Meinzer of the By the Book podcast. You guys gave me the motivation I needed.

Thank you to Lydia Warren for your insight and support and to Becky Hamm for teaching me about personal finance in my brokest days and making my website beautiful.

Thank you to my mom and dad for your encouragement and support (and thanks for the close edits, Dad!) and to Anne and Laura, my best cheerleaders.

Thank you, Darius. You are the best and I am the luckiest.

About the author

Kate Anania is an environmental and economic policy analyst with a strong appreciation for the world of personal finance. She lives all over the country with her husband, son and two rescue kitties. You can read more of Kate's writing at www.twentiesinyourpocket.com.

Made in the USA
Las Vegas, NV
19 January 2023

65839544R10109